THE ART OF
FILM

THE ART OF FILM

WORKING ON JAMES BOND, ALIENS, BATMAN AND MORE

TERRY ACKLAND-SNOW with WENDY LAYBOURN

The History Press

Jacket illustrations:
Front: Plans for the Batmobile.
Back: Diagram of the layout for the cable car scene in *On Her Majesty's Secret Service.*

First published 2022

The History Press
97 St George's Place, Cheltenham,
Gloucestershire, GL50 3QB
www.thehistorypress.co.uk

British Library Cataloguing in Publication Data.
A catalogue record for this book is available from the British
Library.

ISBN 978 0 7509 9742 3

Typesetting and origination by The History Press
Printed in Turkey by Imak

**In memory of my brother,
Brian Ackland-Snow,
1940–2013.**

At the time of his death in 2013, my brother Brian hadn't worked for fourteen years due to the cruel illness Alzheimer's Disease. However, his humour, compassion and generosity still shone through. He was a very unselfish man, both in the workplace and as a husband and father.

Brian loved drawing, art and model-making from an early age but, at our father's insistence, he had to complete a carpentry apprenticeship with the family business before he started in design. After this he joined the art department at the Danziger Studio in Elstree as an assistant; his first film was *The Road to Hong Kong* at Shepperton Studios, where he worked for production designer Roger K. Furse.

He went on to work on many films and television programmes from 1962 until he retired, winning an Oscar in 1987 for Best Art Direction, a BAFTA for Best Production Design for *A Room with a View* and a Primetime Emmy for Outstanding Individual Achievement in Art Direction for the miniseries *Scarlett*.

Brian's film and television credits include *Without a Clue*, *A Room with a View*, *Superman III*, *The Dark Crystal*, *McVicar*, *Dracula*, *Death on the Nile*, *Cross of Iron*, *The Slipper and the Rose*, *There's a Girl in My Soup*, *Battle of Britain*, *2001: A Space Odyssey*, *The Quiller Memorandum*, *The Road to Hong Kong*, *The Magnificent Ambersons*, *Animal Farm*, *Kidnapped*, *Scarlett*, *Cadfael*, *The Man in the Brown Suit* and *Hart to Hart*.

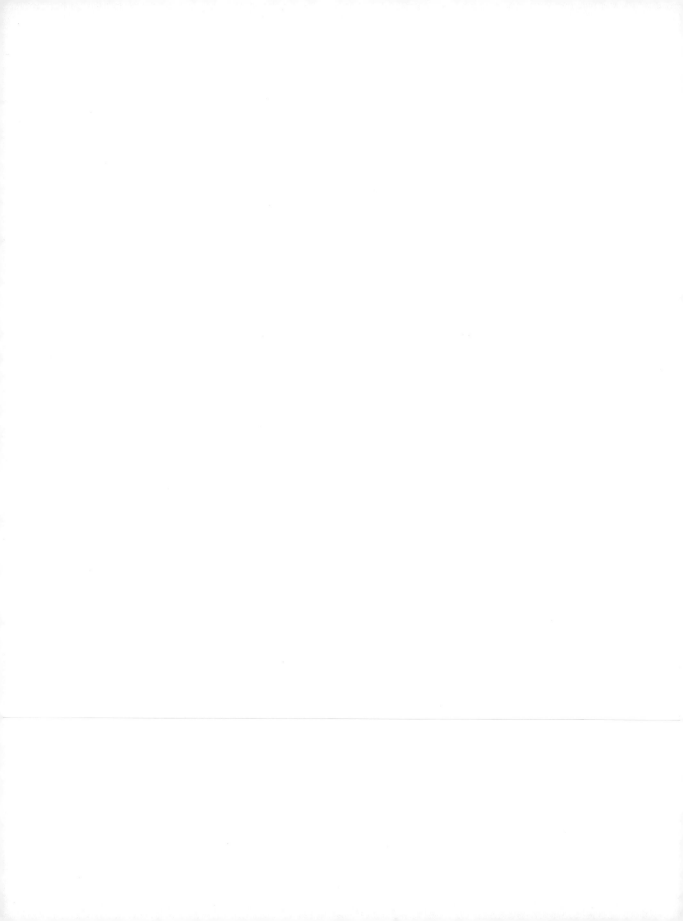

CONTENTS

FOREWORDS

Michael G. Wilson and Barbara Broccoli

Terry's first job for us was draughtsman for *On Her Majesty's Secret Service* (1969) and, several years later, we were lucky to work with him again as an art director on location for *The Living Daylights* (1987), as well as with the late production designer Peter Lamont.

We are delighted that Terry's extensive career has led him to share his film-making passion through his courses at Pinewood Studios, training our next generation of art department creatives.

John Glen

I first met Terry Ackland-Snow when filming *On Her Majesty's Secret Service* and our paths have crossed many times since, lastly on *The Living Daylights*.

When I look back, apart from throwing the best Christmas parties, the art department are the unsung heroes of the Bond movies. I remember filming in the desert and needing a towering bridge to carry away the fleeing horsemen and pursuing tanks. It doesn't rain very much in the desert, so an unimpressive structure across a small wadi was transformed by a foreground miniature into a bridge 90ft high with a silica river flowing beneath.

The miniature was built at Pinewood Studios and transported to Morocco so, with the aid of a nodal head camera mount, we were able to pan and zoom to capture the action taking place on the bridge, together with explosions.

This remains one of my very favourite shots and a lesson to any would-be film director.

Chris Kelly

Making movies for the cinema or television is a team game. No other form of art or entertainment calls for such a wide range of skills. Take a look at a film crew on location and you'll be staggered by the number of vehicles and personnel. Do they really need all those people? Yes, is the answer. Every member of cast and crew has a vital part to play. All the glory goes to actors and directors but where would they be without an army in support? Producers, line producers, writers, directors of photography, lighting, sound recordists, production designers, costume designers, make-up, all with their own mini-departments, props, editors, carpenters, painters, accountants, caterers, drivers … I could go on. Increasingly, over recent decades, an additional creative development has totally transformed the images we see on the screen: VFX (visual special effects generated on computers).

No one in the British film industry is better qualified to take an overview than veteran production designer (art director) Terry Ackland-Snow. Designer of dozens of films, from blockbusters to intimate dramas, he now runs successful courses at Pinewood, passing on with characteristic generosity the techniques he's learned over a long lifetime, which included earning a university doctorate in the process.

It's no secret that in film and TV large egos are not uncommon. Happily, Terry doesn't suffer from one. Having had the privilege of working with him over many years, I can vouch for the fact that he is invariably modest, unflappable, professional and endlessly inventive. In a word, he's the ideal guide.

PREFACE

BY WENDY LAYBOURN

Terry Ackland-Snow has been dealing with the art of illusion for his entire working life and, no, he's not a member of the Magic Circle. He's an art director and production designer in feature film production. Throughout his long career he has worked on more than eighty films and one or two well-known television series since he started in the industry as an apprentice at the age of 16.

In the *Collins English Dictionary*, illusion is defined as a 'deceptive impression of reality' and in film production this definition is more relevant than you would think. The art department follows whatever style is required to construct the right backdrop for the performers and the rest of the production crew to work with, creating the 'illusion' that sets the scene for the audience. Sorry if this spoils your viewing experience but whatever you see on the screen, no matter how real it looks, isn't necessarily what you think it is. It's all down to the smoke and mirrors created by the art director and their team.

Film technology wasn't originally meant to be used for artistic expression but began simply as a commercial extension of live theatrical events, recording the action on stage much like the modern documentary. However, the practitioners soon found that portraying a story on screen was quite different from a theatrical production as there are so many tricks available to film makers that are impossible to achieve on stage.

So, what is an art director? They are essentially the project manager of the art department and work directly for the production designer. They need to have a good eye for decoration and detail and the ability to think visually, to conceptualise ideas and to bring these ideas into tangible form. Not only do they have to use their creative and technical talents in the drawing office but, as they are fully responsible for the construction of the set, they also need a good working knowledge of building materials and architecture, a full understanding of the construction crew's skills and the ability to manage the art department's not inconsiderable budget.

Art directors are artists who can adapt their style to any number of different types of production. They integrate themselves and their team into the mood and feeling of a particular project, whether it is a comedy, a musical, a costume drama or a science-fiction extravaganza. They adapt to the range of materials and the scope of the design, which will test their imagination and skills to the utmost.

Film sets have developed through time from the painted canvas backcloths used in theatres to their present and highly sophisticated form. When film was in its infancy it was essentially just a series of animated photographs but then the showmen stepped in to work with the photographers and began the process of what is now taken for granted as film production.

However, the essence of film making hasn't really changed since those early days. Although the early film makers were working with very basic and unsophisticated equipment and materials, they still managed to create memorable illusions and stunts with simple but often death-defying 'in-camera' effects. The creativity of the modern crew and their passion for telling the story are the same as ever; it's just the technology that has grown over the decades so that the tricks and scenic illusions have become more and more exotic, making the seemingly impossible now a practical reality.

Each year the development of technology and visual processes make film sets more exciting and the learning process never ends. The film crew is like a mobile and ever-changing life force, so even the most experienced art director will find each new project a challenge!

In this book Terry will take you through the stories behind some of the films he has worked on, as well as often explaining how a particular effect or illusion was produced. If you find that you're not quite sure about some of the techniques, check out Chapter 9, where he has described some of the technical stuff in more detail. We hope you enjoy reading this book as much as we've enjoyed putting it together.

Wendy Laybourn

ACKNOWLEDGEMENTS

Within this book we acknowledge all who are sadly no longer with us but who, through their outstanding innovations from the early days of film design to the present day, have left their legacy for the benefit of all film makers.

Special thanks to the following for their contributions: Michael Wilson, Barbara Broccoli, Chris Kelly, John Glen, Robin Vidgeon BSC, Malcolm Stone, Ray Stanley, Emma Farke, Carol Ackland-Snow, Keith Ackland-Snow, Alexandra Kerr, Dusty Symonds and Ann Tricklebank.

Thanks to the following for illustrations:
Warner Brothers: Batmobile
Universal Studios
Henson Productions: Muppet storyboards
MGM: James Bond
Disney Art Department: *Dark Crystal* and *Labyrinth*
EON: *The Living Daylights*
Columbia Pictures: *The Deep*
20th Century Fox: *The Rocky Horror Picture Show*
Paramount Pictures EMI: *Death on the Nile*
Rob Fodder, Propmasters: www.propmasters.net
Leigh Took, Mattes & Miniatures Ltd: www.mattesandminiatures.com
Construction Manager: Terry Apsey
HoD Plasterer: Ken Barley
HoD Painter: Adrian Start
Stills Photographer: Keith Hamshere

TERRY ACKLAND-SNOW'S FILM AND TV CREDITS

Film

Masters of Venus, Richard the Lionheart, The Pink Panther, The Haunting, In the Cool of the Day, The Yellow Rolls-Royce, Carry on Cleo, A Shot in the Dark, Operation Crossbow, The Liquidator, On Her Majesty's Secret Service, Lady 'L', Fahrenheit 451, Eye of the Devil, Blue Max, Half a Sixpence, 2001: A Space Odyssey, The Anniversary, Battle of Britain, Hoffman, Mr Forbush and Penguins, Up Pompeii, The Man Who Had Power Over Women, Papillon, Tommy, The Rocky Horror Picture Show, The Return of the Pink Panther, Barry Lyndon, Sky Riders, The Deep, Death on the Nile, Medusa Touch, Arabian Adventure, Nijinsky, Superman II, The Great Muppet Caper, Dark Crystal, Krull, Superman III, Pirates of Penzance, Supergirl, Spies Like Us, King David, Labyrinth, Aliens, The Living Daylights, Consuming Passions, Batman, Rainbow Thief, Doomsday Gun, Get Real, Bourne Identity, Dad's Army (Original Film), *It's All Happening, The Quest, Puncher's Private Navy, Rocket to the Moon, Take Me High, Rebel Zone* and *Papa*.

Television

The Avengers, Dangerman, Harry's Girls, Black Beauty, Shirley's World, Dick and Julie in Covent Garden, Dopple Clanger, Alternative 3, Inspector Morse Series 2, 3 & 5, *Soldier Soldier* Series 1–6, *Closing Numbers, Kavanagh QC, SOS, Monsignor Renard* and *Without Motive*.

INTRODUCTION

I've worked in film art departments since I was a teenager and I can't tell you how much I've enjoyed it. Thinking back to the amazingly talented people I've worked with and the countries I've worked in, what a very lucky man I am! But how do you condense a career that spans so many films into a readable book? As my job in the art department has always involved a lot of fairly technical and time-consuming work, I thought it best if I sidelined that aspect and just chose a few of the films that I personally found both highly enjoyable and often challenging to work on and which you, the reader, will hopefully recognise from your visits to the cinema – so here goes!

I was the youngest of four brothers: Barry, Brian, my twin Keith (older by 15 minutes) and then me. As a family we weren't very well off but Mum and Dad did a great job bringing us up despite the struggles. I remember one Christmas Dad found a couple of bicycles that had been dumped and set about restoring them. He painted the frames maroon and the wheels silver. The fact that one was a girls' bike and one was a boys' didn't matter to us at all. We were so thrilled with the present.

As youngsters, Keith and I were always up to a bit of mischief. At that time in and around London there were thick fogs called pea-soupers. These were a problem for cars but not so much for us on our bikes as we knew the local roads in north-west London, particularly Long Lane to the A30, like the back of our hands. As our red rear lights were reasonably visible, we decided it would be a good idea to offer to guide the motorists for the princely sum of

6d per mile. This all went very well until we decided to call it a day as we were getting cold and hungry, so we set off towards home. However, we didn't think to tell the drivers, so they followed us all the way to our gate. Dad was not best pleased at having to sort it out!

Dad had worked as a carpenter on such films as *The Thief of Baghdad*, where he made friends with a fellow carpenter called Les Cleaman. When the film work finished and the construction crew were made redundant, he decided to start Ackland-Snow Limited with my Uncle Percy, turning an old chapel in Stanwell into a factory. It had an old-fashioned petrol pump at the front, which was very handy for the company! They took on Les straight away and among the first things they made were oak doors for the local church, before progressing to small sets for the BBC.

I always loved drawing and painting. In front of the factory was a hardware shop, so when I was 11 years old I did a painting of the shops. You can see the factory chimneys in the background.

Les Cleaman left to take up a permanent job with the BBC and was eventually promoted to head of construction there, which enabled him to give Dad more projects. After early jobs building backing in the car park of the chapel for new presenters such as Richard Dimbleby, Dad was given bigger drama sets to work on, such as *Dixon of Dock Green*, *Quatermass* and *The Day of the Triffids*.

Growing up, my twin brother Keith and I used to do small jobs in the factory, such as pulling nails out of wood ready for re-use. We were later promoted to cutting wooden pins for the carpenters to make what were then 'gatelegs', which are folding rostrum legs. For this we were paid 6d an hour – quite a lot for a couple of young lads in those days! We started to work properly in the factory at 16 years old and we were very lucky to have this as a starting point.

Also working at the factory were my other brothers Brian and Barry, the latter of whom sadly died in his 40s of cancer. Brian, four years older than me, was asked to work on a small film at Elstree Studios, with art director Scott McGregor. This was the start of Brian's long and successful career in film. My chance came when Scott McGregor asked Brian to work on another film with him but, as he was already committed to another project, he recommended me. This was my big chance, at 17 or 18 years old, but I must confess I can't remember the name of the film! After that Brian went on to bigger productions, such as *Becket* (1964) with production designer John Bryan and art director Maurice Carter. He eventually won an Oscar for *A Room with a View*.

The studios known as 'Elstree', based in Borehamwood and Elstree in Hertfordshire, have gone through several changes of owner and name over the years since film production began in the area in 1914. At the time it was possibly the largest film and television studio complex outside of the USA and was owned by the Danziger brothers, who specialised in very low-budget features and featurettes, geared primarily to television. You can forgive me for thinking that I'd actually arrived in Hollywood as I walked through the gates for the first time!

From then on I worked on many short films, such as *The Tell-tale Heart* (1960), with art directors Norman G. Arnold and Peter Russell. I went on to a series for television called *Richard the Lionheart* (1962), with a new art director called Roy Stannard.

While I was working on *Richard the Lionheart* I was given a white envelope that, when I opened it, I realised was two weeks' notice. This notice was part of the ACTT[1] union rules but I thought I'd been given the sack. Being a sensitive soul and ever so young, I cried, as I thought I was the only one who'd been given the push. The camera operator could see how upset I was and told me that everyone on the unit got one and they were known as the Chinese handbill! I was so relieved that I could go home and tell my father that this was the normal procedure. However, he already knew what it meant as he had worked as a carpenter on films like *The Thief of Baghdad* and had received one or two of these in his career.

About a week after finishing on *Richard the Lionheart* I went back to Danziger Studios for a visit as I wanted to see what was being filmed. I inadvertently walked into shot wearing a bright yellow anorak – what a dummy! It was a wartime scene with Sherman tanks and a lot

1 Association of Cinematograph, Television and Allied Technicians, now BECTU (Broadcasting, Entertainment, Communications & Theatre Union)

of heavy Second World War vehicles. The set was a one-way street so the vehicles had no room to turn around and they all had to be reversed back to the start. Never would I do that again – a huge lesson learned!

I had a call from an art director called Elliot Scott (Scotty) who was working for MGM and asked if I would like to draw for him. I was delighted so started on the Monday morning at Borehamwood. This was my dream come true. I had to clock in at the gatehouse and on my way to Scotty's office I passed two people going in the opposite direction. They were Elizabeth Taylor and Richard Burton!

However, not all parts of the job were that exciting. I had to work for the studio maintenance engineer, drawing up electrical plumbing diagrams. Thankfully this job only lasted for a few weeks though and I then went on to work on various television series, such as *Dangerman* and *The Cheaters*, as well as many music videos. At last I was working for MGM in the art department in a major studio! I worked there for about three and a half years and I had the good fortune to be mentored by Reg Bream, who was, in my opinion, the best draughtsman at that time. I learned such a lot from him.

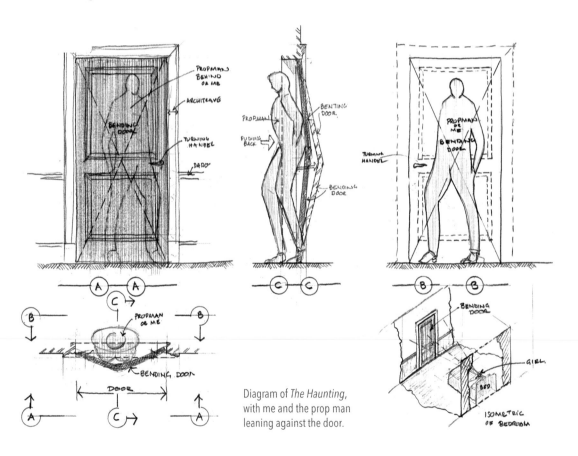

Diagram of *The Haunting*, with me and the prop man leaning against the door.

One film I worked on was *In the Cool of the Day* (1963), starring Peter Fonda. I was so nervous to be working for art director Ken Adam as he was so very well respected but I was lucky I still had Reg Bream alongside me, as well as art director Peter Murton, looking after the locations in Greece.

I later worked with Elliot Scott on many more films, such as *The Yellow Rolls-Royce*, starring Rex Harrison, *A Shot in the Dark*, starring Peter Sellers and Herbert Lom, and *The Haunting*. One of the problems we had with the latter was dealing with the scene where a girl was in bed, looking at the door after hearing heavy footsteps on the landing. The scene was set from her point of view and the door was supposed to start to bend as if something was trying to get in. We had made the door out of pliable PVC so the prop man and I were tasked with leaning on the outside of it to create the right effect. These days I expect it would be the job of the visual effects team to produce this in post-production.

So that was the start of my career. I went on to work on many varied jobs, all of which taught me so much to learn about working in film. After all these years, I'm still learning something new every day.

I'm happy to say that my son Dominic has followed me into the business. I thought he might follow my footsteps into the art department but that was not to be, even though I got him work experience on *Aliens*. He was good enough for the designer, Peter Lamont, to suggest that we take him on permanently, but Dom didn't want that. He said that he wanted to be a carpenter as he loved working with wood, so that was that. He went on to get himself a job with construction manager Terry Apsey and hasn't looked back since. He is now a construction manager in his own right. My daughter Nicola didn't join us in the business – she's a successful illustrator based in Bristol.

My aim in this book is to give you a little insight into a lifetime of working in the film industry from my point of view, with a mixture of both the funny and the tricky incidents, as well as a little explanation every now and again of how we actually created the illusions, with a few sketches and photographs.

When I eventually retired I was very aware of the lack of suitable channels into working in the art department, so in 2001 I set up a specialised training facility at Pinewood Studios, called Film Design International. We have been very successful and to date we have had more than 2,000 students through our doors, many of whom are now working in art departments all over the world.

An essential part of all my courses is to walk the students around the studio so that they absorb the ethos and begin to understand what it is like to work in the feature film environment.

When *Cinderella* (2015) was being filmed, the production designer, Dante Ferretti, was good enough to show my students around the ballroom set, which was built on the 007 Stage. He took the time to explain all about the set and how it was built to encompass the action with all the cameras, lighting and crew.

We noticed there were several large cut-outs of chandeliers hanging and were curious as to why that was. Apparently they were waiting for the real thing from France but had to put something up to work with while they were waiting.

This kind of interaction is invaluable to young people who are eager to make a career in feature film. A guided tour like this introduces them to the construction crews - carpenters, painters, plasterers, riggers, props department and special effects team - who will bring their designs to life.

Everyone involved in film is so proud of their craft and they rarely have a problem in sharing their passion for it with prospective young film makers.

TRAINEE TO DRAUGHTSMAN

THE PINK PANTHER

A SHOT IN THE DARK

THE YELLOW ROLLS-ROYCE

OPERATION CROSSBOW

FAHRENHEIT 451

THE BLUE MAX

HALF A SIXPENCE

ON HER MAJESTY'S SECRET SERVICE

THE BATTLE OF BRITAIN

SHIRLEY'S WORLD

From trainee to junior, I then moved on to the dizzy height of fully fledged draughtsman – which is a generic term in the art department used to describe both male and female practitioners, sometimes referred to as 'drafter' in America. Essentially, the job is more or less the same as in the domestic market but with subtle differences. The art department provides the construction heads of department with all the information they need to build the sets, either in the studio or on location, including a full understanding of what the director and the director of photography require in terms of lighting and camera angles. As each film setting may be in a different era or on another world, they have to be able to adapt the concept very quickly to the demands of the director and the production designer.

The Pink Panther

I got the job on *The Pink Panther* (1963) totally by chance! I was in the bar at Shepperton Studios – the bars in the UK studios used to be the best places to find out which films were hiring – and I got chatting to the designer Peter Mullins, who I knew quite well. He asked what I would like to drink and then asked what I was working on. I said I'd just finished a film and had nothing lined up. He asked if I would like to go to Hong Kong for him as he needed someone there, and of course I said yes! John Comfort was the production manager and he sorted out all the visas and permits so, four days later, I was on the plane. It just shows how useful networking in the studio bars used to be!

When I arrived in Hong Kong there was no filming going on. Blake Edwards and Julie Andrews had gone to Japan, presumably for a break, so we had to wait for them to return. I do remember that there was a lift in the hotel and for one sequence Peter Sellers was to enter the lift surrounded by Chinese stuntmen. During the scene one of the stuntmen broke wind, which set everyone off laughing, including Peter Sellers. He was wearing a peacock-blue satin costume that jiggled when he laughed, which made everyone laugh even more, totally stopping filming.

After about seven takes Blake called me over and said that it was impossible to do the scene as it was. He asked if I thought we could build a replica set in Shepperton when we got back – which of course we did. I brought back all the posters and hotel information that had been in the original lift, so the scene was set again back home exactly as it had been in Hong Kong. This time, too, one of the stuntmen made a noise like breaking wind so the whole giggling thing started again!

Jack Stephens (nicknamed Silver Fox) was the set dresser, or set decorator, depending where you are in the world, and a veteran of so many films. Very often there's confusion about the difference between the responsibility of the dresser and the prop master. The dresser provides non-structural items such as drapes, anything picked up or touched by the performers, 'hero' props that are central to the action (which might be breakaway furniture or glass bottles) as well as mechanicals that might move or be illuminated. The props department deal with anything that might be hired, manufactured or purchased, such as furniture, equipment and machinery. Both departments have to have an extensive knowledge of styles and fashion within different periods globally, from medieval to modern day.

We had a lot of fun in Hong Kong. As you can imagine, there are so many stories from this film. In one scene, a stuntman on a motorbike and sidecar, who was being chased by a black limousine, lost control on the dockside and crashed into a junk that was tied up there. The man who owned it couldn't believe that his home had been smashed but the film company, as always, put everything to rights and he got his home back again as good as new. It was funny seeing the stuntman floating in the dock in his costume. Of course, the bike sank without trace.

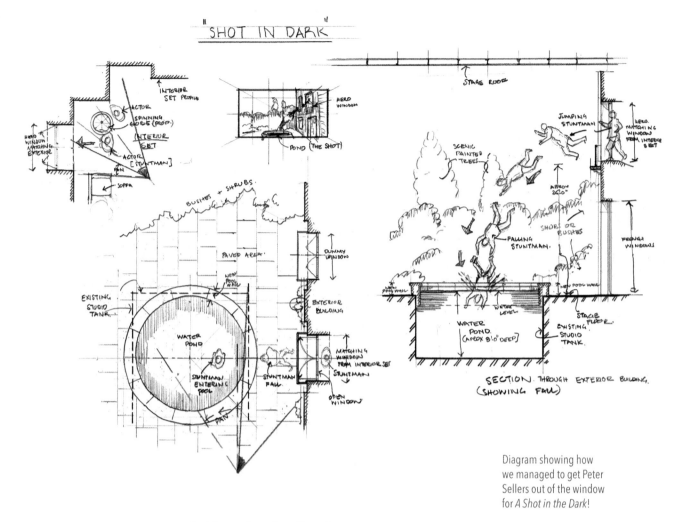

Diagram showing how we managed to get Peter Sellers out of the window for *A Shot in the Dark*!

A Shot in the Dark

I worked with designer Michael Stringer on *A Shot in the Dark* (1964), again with Peter Sellers and Herbert Lom. One scene I remember was when Peter Sellers' character got his hand stuck in the rotating globe, which ended up with him being thrown out of the window. The exterior shot of him flying through the window was a built set in MGM studios at Borehamwood, just outside London. He came out about 25ft up into a fountain – great shot!

Back in the art department, Michael Stringer asked for a card model of the street that we had built. I'd started the model, but when he came into the department, I had only just done the first building. He said that he needed the model in two days and showed me how he wanted it. I learned a lot about making models from him.

Although these days there are very good software packages, three-dimensional cardboard models, built to scale, are still widely used throughout the design process. They help the designer, art director and cinematographer work out the camera angles and where the action is going to take place so that the team doesn't waste any time and money building unnecessary aspects (see Chapter 9 for a more detailed explanation).

The Yellow Rolls-Royce

The Yellow Rolls-Royce (1965) was one of my early films as a draughtsman. It was directed by Anthony 'Puffin' Asquith, who always wore a white boiler suit and was a chain smoker. He also liked to play on a grand piano at lunchtime. There were three art directors – William Kellner, Vincent Korda and Elliot Scott – as the film was made in three sections.

I was working with Elliot on his section. We had to research and draw several aspects of the Royal Ascot Racecourse. We used quite a few miniatures on this film. The car, the yellow Rolls-Royce, was in pristine condition in the early scenes but went slowly downhill once it was being used for all the action shots and escape scenarios in Austria. I remember having to work on a forced perspective backing for a set of the Foreign Office, which Reg Bream helped me with – another new technique learned!

Operation Crossbow

One of the first films I worked on as a junior draughtsman for Elliot Scott at MGM was *Operation Crossbow* (1965). It was such an enjoyable experience. The stars of the film were John Mills, George Peppard, Trevor Howard, Christopher Plummer, Nigel Davenport and my secret passion at the time, Sophia Loren.

Reg Bream was the art director and my job was to draw up the Foreign Office fireplace, the Cabinet Office in 10 Downing Street and the doodlebug (V1), a flying bomb used by the Germans during the Second World War with an engine that cut out when it was about to hit its target, as well as the silent V2 rocket with its mobile launching rig. There were a lot of detailed drawings to do and a lot of research. I drew all the miniatures and all the full-sized pieces. It was very good experience and I learned so much about scale drawings.

Diagram showing how a shot was set up using a foreground miniature for *Operation Crossbow*.

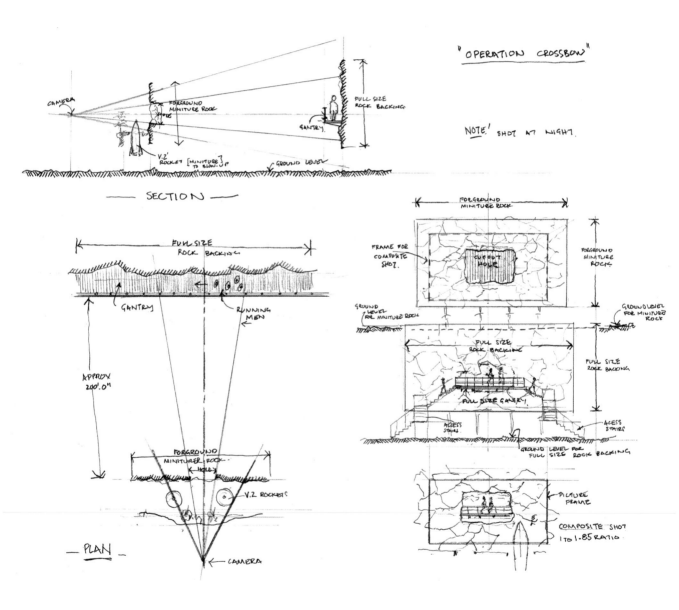

In the film, the German forces had their rockets hidden in giant silos within salt mines, so we had to set up a shot using a foreground miniature. The miniature had a slot cut out to show the rock face 200ft away. We built a full-size rock face with men running in front of it so that through the camera lens it looked as if they were inside the cave.

Miniatures are used in production more than the audience realises. They are extremely detailed models of objects and buildings that can be used to give convincing background detail, or in action sequences when, for various reasons, it is better to use a model than the real object, such as if you have to set a building on fire or blow it up.

Fahrenheit 451

I was a draughtsman on this film; François Truffaut was directing with Alex Thomson as director of photography, Julie Christie starring and designer Tony Walton - who incidentally was married to Julie Andrews at the time - but Syd Cain took over after a while.

One of my jobs was drawing a futuristic fire engine. I visited Dennis Brothers in Guildford, who were specialist manufacturers of fire engines at that time, but I only managed to get fire hoses and a fire bell from them. However, the construction crew did a magnificent job of building the vehicle out of wood - good job it didn't have to move anywhere! I must say that it wasn't my best design but it was a long time ago.

It was filmed mainly at Pinewood Studios, with many of the scenes shot in the extensive woodland that adjoins Pinewood called Black Park and which is used by many productions for all kinds of sequences. For one scene we set up a train carriage as part of a camp set in the woods, surrounded by books - which was part of the story. There were two units filming back to back in Black Park at the time, us and *Carry on up the Jungle* - one a serious drama and one a comedy, it was quite a laugh for both crews.

I also remember I did once set up a helicopter crash in these very woodlands for the television series *Soldier Soldier*. It apparently looked so realistic that dog walkers passing by said that they hadn't heard the crash but they wanted to check everyone was OK!

The Blue Max

Following that I was loaned out to a film called *The Blue Max* (1966). This was set in Ireland and again starred George Peppard but this time the action took place during the First World War. When I first arrived at the location in Ireland it was in thick cloud and, being young and naïve, I couldn't see the point of being there. However, after about three weeks, the clouds lifted and the view was amazing, so I fully understood why this location had been chosen.

Diagram showing the location plan for *The Blue Max*.

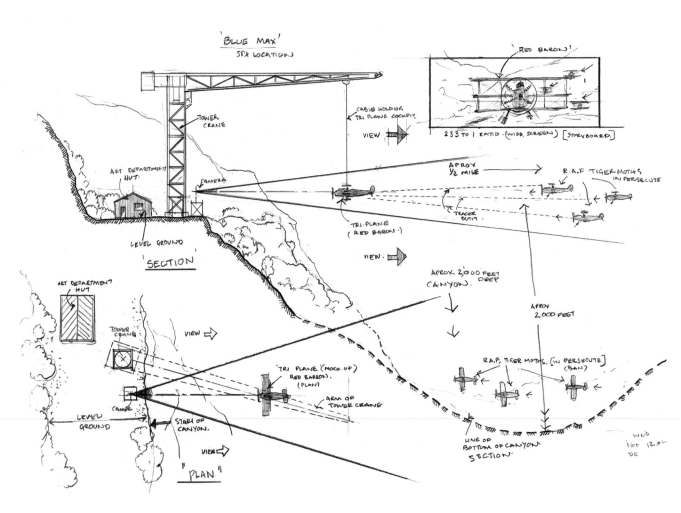

Working for art director Arthur Lawson, I was tasked with looking after all the special effects shots, which included a triplane cockpit mock-up hanging from a tower crane in the mountains. It was very exciting, as I'd never done anything like it before! The mock-up was designed to simulate the plane being 2,000ft up with thirty-five biplanes from the Royal Flying Corps chasing it. There was a bit of a hairy moment when the cockpit caught fire with George Peppard in it and it took some time to get him to safety but thankfully no one was hurt. I wonder what today's Health and Safety would have to say about that!

I was loaned out during this time to many other films in various studios. Particularly exciting for me was a Bond film in Pinewood for designer Syd Cain, as this was where I drew my first major set. I must have done reasonably well as, on completion of the film, Syd called me into his office and asked me if I would join him on another film in a month's time. Naturally I said, 'Yes.' He mentioned that it would pay a lot more than I was getting at the time, so I gave in my notice. It was a big decision but unfortunately the new film collapsed. Happily it wasn't long before I was working again though!

Following that I went to Birmingham to work on a film called *Brumburger* for designer Reese Pemberton and set dresser Mike Ford. The three of us had a publicity photograph taken in which our heads were supposed to be coming out of paint tins. Although the film starred Cliff Richard, I don't think it got much coverage and I doubt that many people have heard of it. Many years later I was in Hong Kong working with a producer who had worked on a television programme called *Clapperboard*. To my surprise, he said that he had heard of it – thank God someone had!

I worked on a number of British films, such as *Up Pompeii!* at EMI Studios, starring Frankie Howerd. He was such a funny man and the filming had to stop so often as he made the unit laugh so much they couldn't continue. I also worked on *The Anniversary*, starring Bette Davis. Miss Davis was, to say the least, a little difficult to work with. The original director was Alvin Rakoff, who was fairly quickly replaced by Roy Ward Baker (as Miss Davis didn't get on with Alvin's ideas), and Reese Pemberton was production designer. I didn't enjoy that experience too much but it was good practice in dealing with difficult people!

A few years later I worked with designer Tony Masters on *Mr. Forbush and the Penguins* (1971), sometimes called *Cry of the Penguins*, building a replica of Shackleton's hut. I then went on to a Peter Sellers film called *Hoffman*. It was an incredibly boring film for us to work on as it was all done on one set, but it was a job!

Half a Sixpence

The musical *Half a Sixpence* (1967) starred Tommy Steele, a pop legend of the time, and was directed by George Sidney. This was the first film where I was able to stand by the camera, next to the operator Kelvin Pike and the lovely director of photography Geoffrey Unsworth (winner of two Oscars and five BAFTAs). It was a very exciting and educational experience! The designer was an American called Ted Haworth and the art director was Peter Murton.

We were shooting on the riverbank near Henley-on-Thames and we had built a jetty, painted white for a scene. On the morning of the shoot Derek Cracknell, the first assistant, couldn't find the jetty. When we went down to the site we found that it hadn't disappeared but was underwater as the river, which is tidal at that point, had risen during the night. In a panic, Derek sent me downriver to the lock keeper to ask him if he could let the water through the weir so that they could continue shooting. The lock keeper was very accommodating but said that if he did that, he would flood Marlow, the next town downriver – not a great idea!

Another problem we faced was an idea that the director had for Tommy Steele to be rowing in a puddle whilst singing. I think the song went something like, 'If it's got to rain let it be Monday, Tuesday, Wednesday, any day but Sunday'. The problem was that we were in a field on the riverbank with no puddles in sight! I contacted the art department to ask them how we could do it. Bob Cartwright, the assistant art director, came up with the idea to make shallow holes in the field, line them with cement and paint them the same green as the grass. The cement was delivered and Bob organised the loan of a punt – which has a flat bottom – so once we had made the puddles, Tommy Steele could do his rowing and singing. The scene

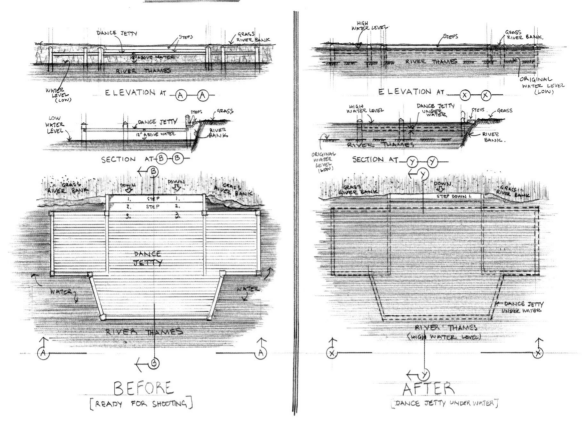

"HALF A SIXPENCE" RIVER THAMES HENLY-ON-THAMES [LOCATION]

BEFORE
[READY FOR SHOOTING]

AFTER
[DANCE JETTY UNDER WATER]

Sketch of the 'flooding' dance jetty we built for *Half a Sixpence*.

looks so easy on screen but it took so much work and organisation to put it all together!

The pier and beach scenes were in Eastbourne, with horses and carriages on the promenade. However, in the period of the film the promenade wasn't paved, so the director said we had to lose the paving. I didn't know what to do as I was on my own at the time. I quickly rang Ted Haworth, who was in London, for advice and he told me to dampen the pavement down and throw tons of peat over it. We had the fire brigade handy so they did the damping down while I went to find the peat. I thought that they might just use a small hose but no, there they were with the full-on water jet! Once most of the water had drained away we spread the peat over the paving. The peat stuck to the wheels of the carriages, which was a bit of a nightmare, but it all worked well in the end! Thank goodness for the construction crew, who are the mainstay of any production.

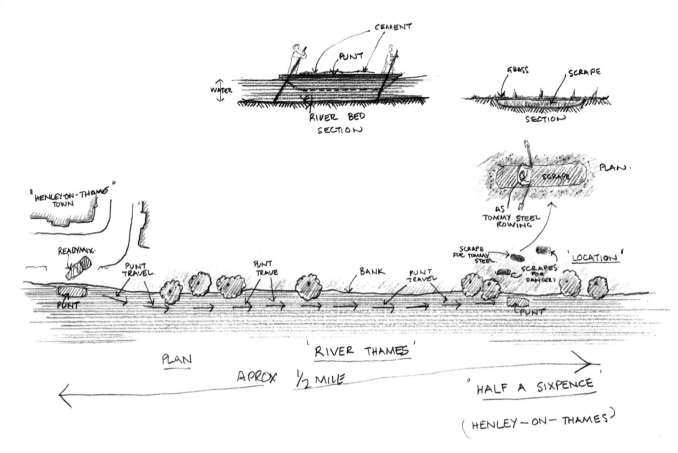

Without this extremely creative and talented workforce – generally around 200 on a large feature film – the actors would be doing their lines in an empty sound stage.

Diagram of the set-up in Henley for the rowing scene in *Half a Sixpence*.

On Her Majesty's Secret Service

On Her Majesty's Secret Service (1969) was the first Bond film I worked on. The designer was Syd Cain, working with set dresser Peter Lamont and camera operator Alec Mills. The location was the Alpine Room in a restaurant called Piz Gloria in Mürren-Schilthorn in Switzerland, 10,000ft up a mountain. You could only reach it by cable car and it felt like I was on the top of the world!

I was on location for the prep work, not for the actual shoot, but I do remember drawing up the cable car as a set piece at Pinewood for a fight scene, as well as the main rock set. If I remember rightly it was built on E Stage at Pinewood.

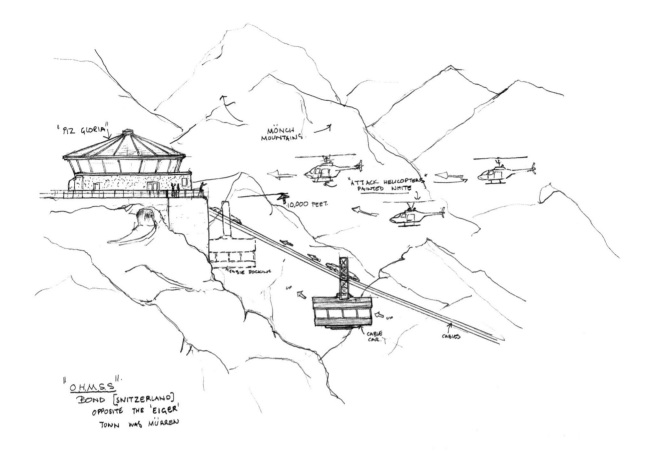

Within the image: "PIZ GLORIA", MÖNCH MOUNTAINS, "ATTACK HELICOPTERS" PAINTED WHITE, 10,000 FEET, CABLE DOCKING, UP, UP, CABLE CAR, CABLES, "O.H.M.S.S." BOND [SWITZERLAND] OPPOSITE THE 'EIGER' TOWN WAS MÜRREN

Diagram of the layout for the cable car scene in *On Her Majesty's Secret Service*.

The Battle of Britain

For *The Battle of Britain* (1969) I worked with the special physical effects unit. The sequences involved filming pilots in the cockpits of planes such as the Spitfire and the Heinkel. The cockpit with the actor was a rig set before a front-projection screen and the Spitfire had to be foreshortened. I worked on this with draughtsmen John Fenner, Dennis Bosher and Frank Wilson, and art director Bert Davey. We also had to foreshorten the Heinkel III and the Messerschmitt.

Front projection is a system where the foreground action is placed in front of a moving background plate or painting. It involves tricky mirror and lens set-ups but hopefully the audience will never be aware that it exists.

I worked on this film for a year and enjoyed it very much, although I would have liked to have spent some time with the main unit.

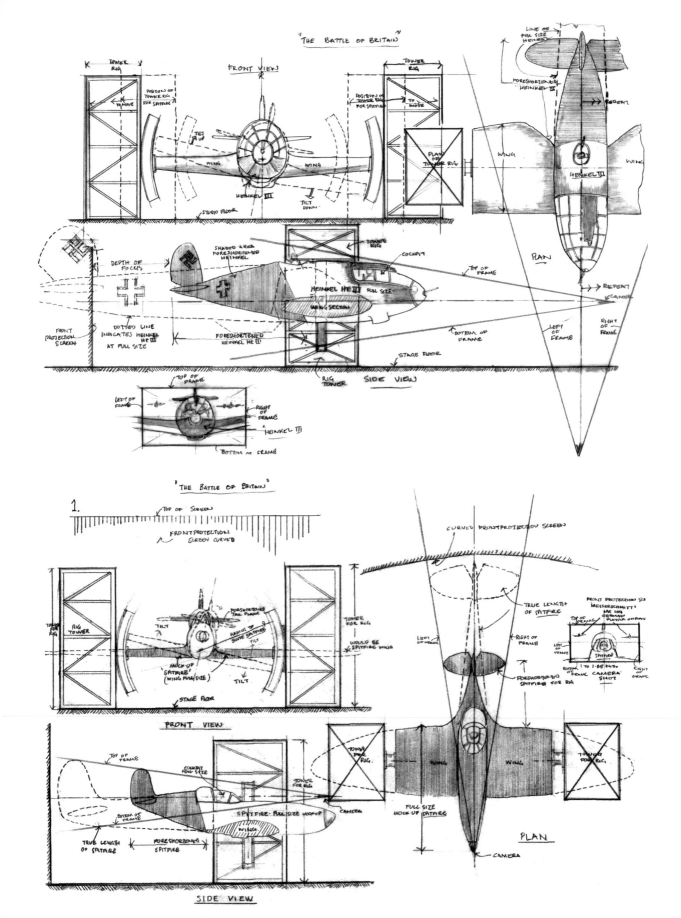

"THE BATTLE OF BRITAIN"

FRONT VIEW

TOWER RIG

TOWER RIG

POSITION OF TOWER RIG FOR SPITFIRE

TO MOVE

POSITION OF TOWER RIG FOR SPITFIRE

TO MOVE

TILT UP

PLAN OF TOWER RIG

WING

WING

HEINKEL III

TILT DOWN

STUDIO FLOOR

LINE OF FULL SIZE HEINKEL

FORESHORTENED HEINKEL III

REPEAT

WING

WING

HEINKEL III

PLAN

DEPTH OF FOCUS

SHADED AREA FORESHORTENED HEINKEL

TOWER RIG

COCKPIT

TOP OF FRAME

HEINKEL HE III FULL SIZE

WING SECTION

REPEAT (CAMERA)

FRONT PROJECTION SCREEN

DOTTED LINE INDICATES HEINKEL HE III AT FULL SIZE

FORESHORTENED HEINKEL HE III

BOTTOM OF FRAME

STAGE FLOOR

RIG TOWER

LEFT OF FRAME

RIGHT OF FRAME

SIDE VIEW

TOP OF FRAME

LEFT OF FRAME

RIGHT OF FRAME

HEINKEL III

BOTTOM OF FRAME

"THE BATTLE OF BRITAIN"

1.

TOP OF SCREEN

FRONT PROJECTION SCREEN CURVED

CURVED FRONT PROJECTION SCREEN

TRUE LENGTH OF SPITFIRE

FORESHORTENED TAIL PLANE

TILT

RADIUS TO SUITE SPITFIRE TILT

TOWER FOR RIG

WOULD BE SPITFIRE WING

RIG TOWER

TOWER FOR RIG

MOCK-UP SPITFIRE (WING FULL SIZE)

TILT

STAGE FLOOR

FRONT VIEW

FRONT PROJECTION SCR MESSERSCHMITT ME 109 GERMAN PLAYING COMING

TOP OF FRAME

LEFT OF FRAME

RIGHT OF FRAME

SPITFIRE

BOTTOM OF FRAME

1 TO 1.85 RATIO CAMERA SHOT

RIGHT OF FRAME

LEFT OF FRAME

RIGHT OF FRAME

FORESHORTENED SPITFIRE FOR RIG

TOP OF FRAME

TOWER FOR RIG

CAMERA

FULL SIZE MOCK UP SPITFIRE

WING

WING

TOWER FOR RIG

PLAN

TOP OF FRAME

COCKPIT FULL SIZE

BOTTOM OF FRAME

SPITFIRE FULL SIZE MOCK-UP

WING

TRUE LENGTH OF SPITFIRE

FORESHORTENED SPITFIRE

CAMERA

SIDE VIEW

Opposite:
Top: Diagram of the
Heinkel build for *The
Battle of Britain*.
Bottom: Diagram of the
Spitfire build for *The Battle
of Britain*.

Shirley's World

Shirley's World (1971) was a television series starring Shirley MacLaine, with production designer John Blezard and assistant art director Tony Reading. We were filming in Wales on a beach and, as they were short of an extra, they asked me to stand in and row two actors in a small boat across to the beach dressed as a Second World War soldier, complete with steel helmet. An unexpected wave hit the side of the boat, so it capsized. It was only a few feet of water but we all went under, still being filmed. So there I was, caught on camera with my helmet having slipped halfway down my face, filled with water, and covering my mouth and nose. I thrashed around, thinking I was drowning! Shirley and the crew were on the shore laughing helplessly as I must have looked so silly.

Setting up the shot for the dreaded rowing boat scene in *Shirley's World*.

For another scene we needed a lamb, which we were to borrow from the local farmer. The only problem was that it was in a small hut with its fairly large and aggressive mother. Trying to separate a lamb from its mum isn't at all easy but John said that he would take the lamb if I would fend off the ewe. We had a bit of a scuffle so the hut collapsed and she escaped, chasing John with her lamb. I still see that series on television in hotel rooms and it surprises me that it's still being aired!

DRAUGHTSMAN
TO ART DIRECTOR
TO PRODUCTION DESIGNER

PAPILLON

THE ADVENTURES OF BLACK BEAUTY

JULIE AND DICK AT COVENT GARDEN

BARRY LYNDON

TOMMY

THE ROCKY HORROR PICTURE SHOW

Papillon

Opposite: Plan of the dormitory for the prisoners.

Out of the blue one day I had a call from production designer Tony Masters asking me if I was prepared to spend a long period of time on location in Jamaica. Of course I said that I would love to do that so, quick as a flash, I was on the Jamaica Airways flight from Heathrow and nine hours later I was in Jamaica.

The film was *Papillon* (1973) and it was my first long stint on location. I had never been in the tropics so it was an exciting experience. Les Tomkins, Jim Morahan and Alan Roderick-Jones were with me as draughtsmen, working for art director Jack Maxsted. Incidentally, this was my first encounter with fireflies – amazing!

Les was there for a week before I arrived and Dick Frift, the construction manager, was busy setting up his workshops. Jack had set up the base for the art department in a small studio near Montego Bay.

One really strange thing that happened to me and Les Tomkins was that we were held hostage for a day by a group of locals who wanted to work as security on the film. Happily, the producer agreed and we were released.

When we got back, a local lady who was working in the production office suggested that we should carry guns for protection but a colleague in the art department called Jim said that the only protection we would need would be plane tickets to London! It just goes to show, when you're working in film and travelling all around the world anything can happen!

The main set was the penal colony where the characters, played by Steve McQueen and Dustin Hoffman, were incarcerated. It was built on two football pitches in a place called Falmouth. Les had done the main layout and we each had a section of the prison to work on. I had the dormitory and the prison cells, which we had to match precisely with the original cells in the notorious Devil's Island in French Guiana. The cells were to be built in the studio complex, not on the Falmouth site. As well as having to reference the original bars of the cells, I had to work it out so that Steve McQueen would be seen from different camera angles through the bars but without blocking any part of the image – more difficult than you would think!

Opposite: Ground plan of the prison.

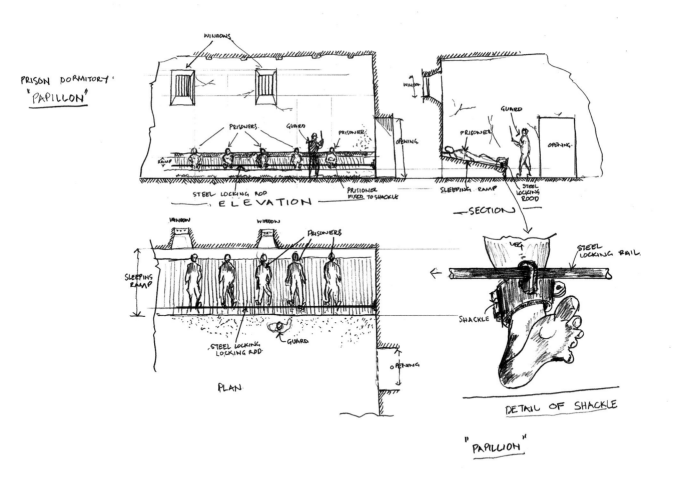

PRISON DORMITORY:
"PAPILLON"

WINDOWS

PRISONERS   GUARD   PRISONER

RAMP   STEEL LOCKING ROD   PRISONER FIXED TO SHACKLE   OPENING

E L E V A T I O N

WINDOW   GUARD   PRISONER   OPENING

SLEEPING RAMP   STEEL LOCKING ROOD

— SECTION —

WINDOW   WINDOW   PRISONERS

SLEEPING RAMP

STEEL LOCKING LOCKING ROD   GUARD   OPENING

PLAN

LEG   STEEL LOCKING RAIL.

SHACKLE

DETAIL OF SHACKLE

"PAPILLON"

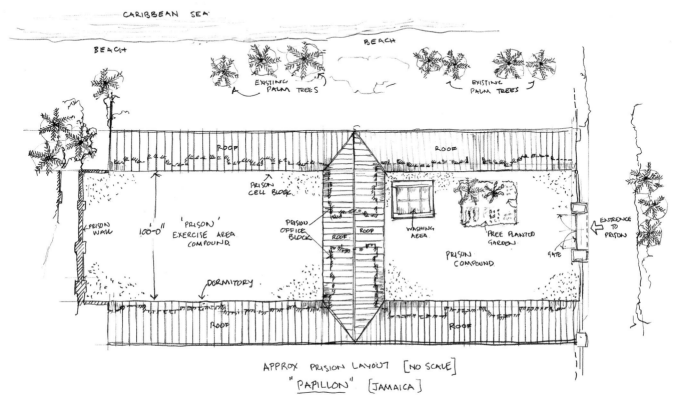

CARIBBEAN SEA

BEACH   BEACH

EXISTING PALM TREES   EXISTING PALM TREES

ROOF   ROOF

PRISON CELL BLOCK

100'-0"   'PRISON' EXERCISE AREA COMPOUND.

PRISON WALL

PRISON OFFICE BLOCK   ROOF   ROOF

WASHING AREA   TREE PLANTED GARDEN

PRISON COMPOUND.

ENTRANCE TO PRISON

GATE

DORMITORY

ROOF   ROOF

APPROX PRISION LAYOUT [NO SCALE]
"PAPILLON" [JAMAICA]

The finished prison.

On set in Falmouth there was a scene where Dustin Hoffman's character was tending the garden. The garden had to have banana plants in it, which apparently are a bit tricky to move and re-plant as they tend to go limp, so they have to be allowed to settle down naturally. This meant that the garden had to be planted first, with the set being gradually built around it.

On this film, there was one set that stood out from the rest. Built on the dockside, it was the interior of the prison ship that transported the inmates to the island. The prisoners in transit would be in the hold and the director, Frank Schaffner, wanted the ship to appear to hit rough seas. As there were no portholes in the hold, the sea and heavy waves wouldn't be visible, so that made it a little easier to design. We built the structure on a rostrum about 5ft from the ground on what you could only describe as upside-down roof trusses. It was fixed by bungee straps and held level by legs. When the legs were removed you could then rock the set from side to side, giving the impression of the ship being in rough sea, with the hammocks and lights swinging back and forth authentically. Although I'd love to say I was a genius and thought all this out by myself, as with every other aspect of making a film, it was a team effort: we put our heads together to make it work.

Clockwise from above: Me with Dick Frift (holding the bananas) and Alan Roderick-Jones just messing about!; On set during the construction; The beautiful area we were living and working in.

Me, Les Tomkins and Jim Morahan measuring up for the yellow fever hospital.

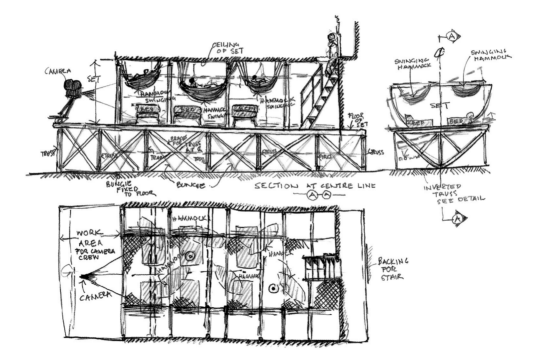

Diagrams showing how we managed to make the prison ship on the dockside rock authentically.

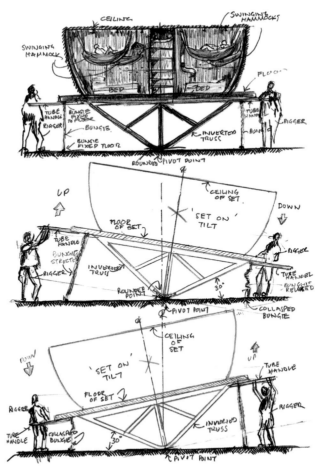

Jim and I rented a villa close to the studio for the duration of the shoot. It was big enough that our families could come out and visit and we had a full complement of staff – cook, cleaner and gardener. We had a great time. The children went to school so there was no interruption to their education and, as we were there over the Christmas period, they did very well for presents from the crew! Going Christmas shopping was very odd as the shops were all done out with snow scenes and Christmas carols sung by the Salvation Army – and all with the temperature at 40°C!

I wanted to work on the next Bond film, which was also set in Jamaica, but *Papillon* went on so long that I was still working on it when Bond started so, regretfully, I had to pass on that.

The Adventures of Black Beauty

I was employed as a set dresser on the 1973 television series *The Adventures of Black Beauty*, which was filmed on a farm between Harefield and Rickmansworth in the Outer London area.

As anyone who has had anything to do with horses knows, no matter how well trained they are, they don't always care to do certain things. This is why there were five horses used throughout the show, supplied by the horse master Reg Dent. One was very good at galloping free on command wherever it was needed, field, beach or woodland. One could stand quietly posing for periods of time, one was quite happy walking through the house without getting spooked, and so on. In the book, the horse Black Beauty was very distinctive: jet black with a white star on his face. However, all of these horses were very different in colour and markings so, like all superstars, they had to go through hair and make-up every time they were needed!

In the drawing office on site for *The Adventures of Black Beauty*.

On the set of *The Adventures of Black Beauty* at Stocker's Farm, Harefield. You can just see Black Beauty's ears in the gap between the barns!

Julie and Dick at Covent Garden

This was a television movie musical directed by Blake Edwards, starring Julie Andrews and Dick van Dyke. Blake Edwards wanted an art director who'd worked in feature film so he asked me. He was only able to work with a single camera on this production and he also wanted to be on the stage directing the performers. Normally, with television, the director works from the booth with monitors but that didn't suit Blake at all.

The designer was Peter Roden. We got on well together and I really enjoyed the job. The set was built off site and then erected in Elstree Studios; television was a very different way of working for me.

It was through working on this movie that I was fortunate enough to meet the legendary John Wayne! I was with the producer Peter Roden and we had to go back to his office through the bar, where I caught sight of John Wayne having his lunch. I believe he was a guest on *The Muppets* at the time. I was a fan and had seen him in many films so Peter asked if I would like to meet him. Peter went over to his table, had a word and beckoned me over. I couldn't believe that I was going to meet one of my heroes. Who didn't like a John Wayne western? He stood up to his full height and, my word, he was a very tall man. He shook my hand and his one hand was bigger than my two hands put together. I had met John Wayne, the Duke. I'll never forget that day!

Barry Lyndon

On Stanley Kubrick's *Barry Lyndon* (1975) I worked for art director Roy Walker and designer Ken Adam – what a privilege! The art department won an Oscar and a BAFTA for this film.

I went with Ken Adam and Stanley Kubrick to Ireland to look at locations. We had a map divided into a 5-mile-square grid pinned to a board so that we could cover each area separately. We had taken 10in x 8in black-and-white photographs of each area, which we had also pinned to the board.

My claim to fame was that I found Huntington Castle, which was eventually used, as well as the tree under which Barry Lyndon (played by Ryan O'Neal) and the heroine first meet. Bert from the construction department and I went to check out the castle. On the way we called into the village shop in Clonegal to ask for directions and wondered why we got some funny looks, but the shopkeeper told us it was just up the road so off we went.

When we got there we were invited to have a look around by the owner, Mr Durdin Robertson. He took us into an oak-panelled room with a roaring fire in the hearth, suits of armour and a few cobwebs hanging about. It was just what we were looking for. Then he said to come and meet his sister. She looked a bit scary dressed in a big black cloak.

She invited us upstairs to see more of the castle and we noticed that all the doors in the corridor were painted black with a flame-red symbol. We went into one of the rooms and saw that everything was black, including the big four-poster bed. When she mentioned that this was their initiation room as part of their black-magic practices, we said, 'Very nice,' and were out of there quick as a flash.

Our hostess then invited us up into the loft to see their collection of doll's houses, just in case we might want to use them as props, and down to the basement, which had a lovely vaulted ceiling. She told us that a maid had been murdered there and that you could often hear her crying. By this time Bert was hanging on to me like his life depended on it and I wasn't feeling too brave either.

They asked us to stay for lunch. It was probably the last thing we wanted to do but we had been given strict instructions to be very polite, so we went with them into the dining room. The fireplace slid to one side – more drama – but it was only a hidden door leading to the kitchen, and once the food trolley had been pushed through, it slid back again!

During lunch I couldn't help but mention that their lifestyle was a little 'unusual', at which point our hosts laughed and said that the whole black-magic thing was a tourist attraction and they were doing very well encouraging Americans to visit. There was apparently a deal where, if anyone could spend more than two nights in the place without freaking out, they could have a discount! They had also constructed a 'Temple of Isis', which is apparently a tourist attraction to this day.

We couldn't wait to get back and tell Stanley Kubrick and Roy Walker that they had to check it out for themselves, secretly hoping they would get the same treatment! In the end the castle was used for the scene where John Quinn (Leonard Rossiter) courted Nora Brady (Gay Hamilton).

One day, Stanley Kubrick and Ken Adam came to my area in the art department. Just beyond my window was an oast house that had been dressed ready for filming and I told them that the set was ready to view. Ken was happy to go and view the actual set but Stanley wanted me to make a white-card model. Foolishly I asked how big he would like it. 'Big enough to get my head into' was the response, and I thought, *Oh, that big*! Normally a card model would be small scale so that the director and the cinematographer could plan the shots. It seemed silly to me that, as the actual set was only a few strides away, a model had to be made at all; however, he was the boss so I did as he asked. When finished, the model had a side that could

be taken away so he could put his head in. He came, stuck his head inside the model and looked around for what seemed like five minutes, withdrew his head and said to Ken, 'OK, let's look at the set now.' That's film making!

For a particular scene Stanley wanted around 700 soldiers with fixed bayonets, charging and then stopping every 20yd, still perfectly lined up. The scene was to be filmed in two adjoining fields and the camera track was 700ft long. so a hedgerow had to be removed to accommodate the shot.

The owner of Huntingdon Castle, Mr Durdin Robertson, dressed up to receive overseas visitors to the 'Temple of Isis'.

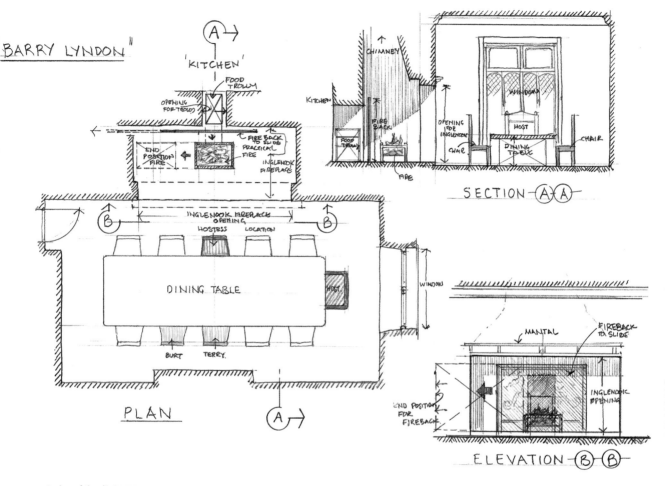

"BARRY LYNDON"

'KITCHEN'

FOOD TROLLY

OPENING FOR TROLLY

FIRE BACK TO SLIDE PRACTICAL FIRE

END POSITION FIRE

INGLENOOK FIREPLACE

INGLENOOK FIREPLACE OPENING

HOSTESS   LOCATION

DINING TABLE

HOST

BURT   TERRY

PLAN

CHIMNEY

KITCHEN

FIRE BACK

FOOD TROLLY

FIRE

OPENING FOR INGLENOOK

CHAIR

WINDOW

HOST

DINING TABLE

CHAIR

SECTION A A

WINDOW

MANTAL

FIREBACK TO SLIDE

END POSITION FOR FIREBACK

INGLENOOK OPENING

ELEVATION B B

A plan of the dining room showing the moving fireplace.

The problem was how to make sure that the soldiers were in perfect order every time they halted. Stanley himself came up with the solution: 6in squares of hardboard painted green, fixed with spikes to the ground, for each soldier to stand on at the end of the charge. It was a really clever and simple idea that worked remarkably well. It saved so much time on the shoot, but what a back-aching job we had putting them all in place!

Tommy

Tommy (1975) was the first time I worked on a film with so many music legends. It was written by The Who and starred them, Elton John and Eric Clapton – as well as Oliver Reed and Ann-Margret. The director was Ken Russell, the designer Paul Dufficy, and the art director John Clark, with me as assistant art director.

There was a famous scene on a theatre stage with Elton John performing 'Pinball Wizard' wearing extremely high and ornate platform boots. I took the boots home afterwards to show my family. I put them on outside and walked in and my wife almost passed out with shock seeing me so tall! However, I had a bit of a problem as I couldn't get them off without falling down to the ground. I didn't think it was at all funny but they all did If only I'd kept them I'd be a very rich man now.

A plan of the stage and set layout for *Tommy*.

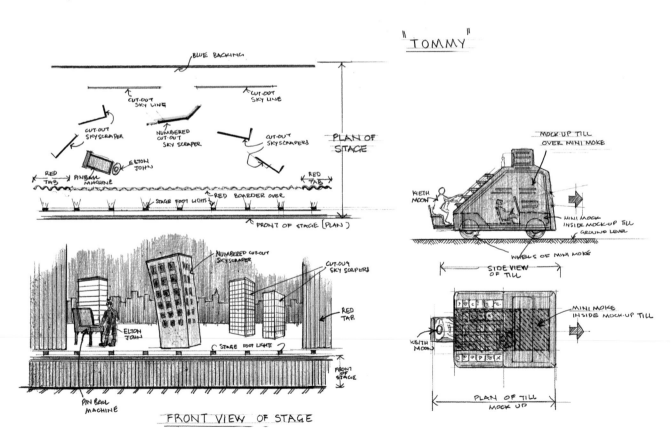

For another scene we had to build a vehicle that looked like an oversized cash till, which Keith Moon was to drive into Dover Castle. We based it on a Mini Moke and it was such a lot of fun to build but I must say it did look very odd.

John Clark was asked by Ken Russell to do a small cameo shot with Ann-Margret, where he said something like, 'It's a boy, Mrs Robinson, it's a boy!' I helped John rehearse his line but, when it came to shooting it, Ken Russell shouted, 'Stop! Stop! You have to sing it!' John replied that he couldn't sing a note, but he didn't let that stop him. It's well worth trying to spot that moment in the film.

The Rocky Horror Picture Show

Straight after finishing on *Tommy*, John Clark was asked to work on a film called *The Rocky Horror Picture Show*. He asked me to join him again as assistant art director, shooting in Bray Studios near Windsor, and of course I jumped at the chance.

The studio complex at Bray included Oakley Court, an old manor house which is famous for being the base of the Hammer Horror series of films. They made their final film there in 1966 but the studios continued to be in use for several years afterwards, for the *St. Trinian's* series, the 1970s *Doctor Who* series, Gerry Anderson's *Space: 1999* and many others.

The designer was Brian Thomson, who had worked on the stage show. However, once preparation had started, Brian said he was leaving to work on the Broadway stage production, so John was asked to take his place. He asked if I would take over as art director – naturally I did!

A week later John took me to one side and said that he also had to leave. He had a new architectural practice in Tottenham Court Road in London and his licence to practise had just come through so he was eager to get started. I wondered who was going to be the new designer and he said that 'them upstairs' were discussing options right now.

I was called 'upstairs' to see the director Jim Sharman and the producer Michael White and they informed me they'd decided on the designer.

'Good,' I said. 'Who is it?'

'It's you, you fool. Do you want it or not?'

After a moment's thought, I said, 'Of course I do!'

I was only 29 years old and hadn't really taken into account that it wasn't just designing I was going to have to do. I had to manage budgets and schedules, get the whole of the art department crew together and find locations. It was truly a baptism of fire and a massive learning experience!

Under the circumstances I thought it would be a good idea if I had a really experienced construction crew to work with so I rang Dick Frift from *Papillon* for advice. He said he knew someone he would recommend and who was available. After a slight pause he said, 'Me, you fool! I haven't worked for four months and I can start tomorrow with a full construction crew.' I don't think I've been called 'fool' to my face so many times before or since that film! Dick helped me so much with the construction budget and I learned such a lot from him. As he had worked on many types of film and as this wasn't such a huge budget, I was so lucky to have him on my side helping me through.

Now, who could I have as my art director? It was a big jump from starting the film as assistant art director to becoming the designer and looking for an art director to work for me! Dick suggested Norman Dorme. Oddly I had phoned him a few weeks earlier asking for a job. When I called him again, he told me that he also hadn't worked for months and he agreed to come on the film, so my luck was in again. He was such a great asset and he went on to work with me on other films all over the world.

The laboratory set was quite challenging. The script featured a wall of death ride on a motorbike with Meat Loaf as the rider but it was decided that it was a bit too dangerous, so I designed a ramp with the motorbike bursting out of a large fridge, which would be safer. This set-up was agreed, along with the colours of red and pink for the walls. The pink tiles were made out of hardboard squares with the different shades at random on the walls. The freezer indicated on the plan and the elevation is where the performer rode the motorbike out of the freezer. We frosted both bike and actor with wax, which looked very effective. On this set we also had the Narrator crashing through the wall. It was quite a challenge but Norman was a great help.

Opposite: Plan and sketch of Frank -N-Furter's laboratory in *The Rocky Horror Picture Show*, showing the freezer ramp down which the motorcycle ridden by Meat Loaf enters the set.

INT.
"FRANK'S LABORATORY"

THE ROCKY HORROR
PICTURE SHOW

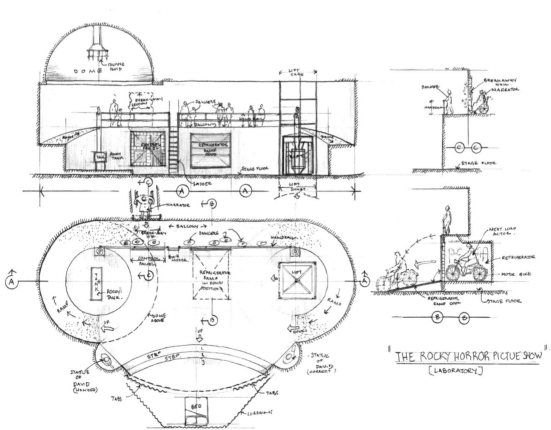

"THE ROCKY HORROR PICTURE SHOW"
[LABORATORY]

In one scene Brad, Janet and the Narrator had to turn into stone statues. We had to do a body cast of the actors, which was quite simple – but the Narrator was in a wheelchair, so Dick suggested that we spray him and the wheelchair in plaster. It worked and he looked like stone, although I'm not sure it was very comfortable!

One set was the Transylvanian Theatre with a swimming pool on the stage. Richard O'Brien, the writer, requested that we use deck chairs for the audience to sit on. Set dresser Ian Whittaker had got some old theatre seating that we were going to use and which I thought looked good – but no, Richard wanted deck chairs, so that was that. We had all the deck chairs covered with red-and-white-striped material with a red carpet down the centre and it worked well, even though I say so myself.

Plan of the swimming pool in the Transylvanian Theatre.

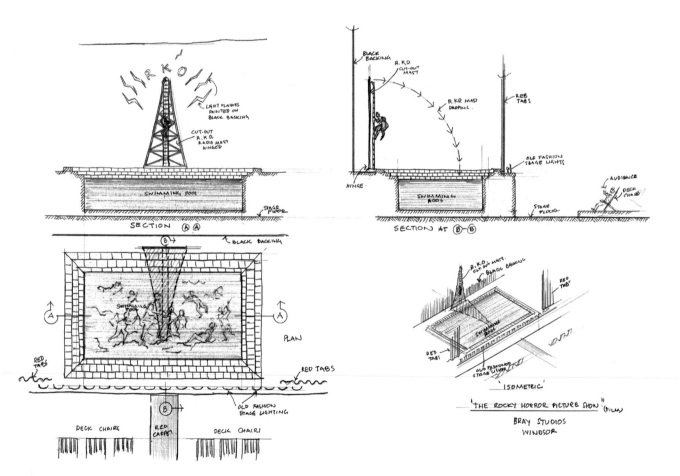

The actual swimming pool was designed to suit the camera aspect ratio – essentially how the camera lens would see it. At the bottom of the pool was a Michelangelo-style painting done by scenic artist Robert Spencer, and Rocky was to hit the water, disturbing the painting.

All in all it was an exciting and memorable film to work on. At the time the production was considered to be fairly small but, of course, it's now a cult movie. There was a shot that parodied the 1939 painting *American Gothic* by Grant Wood, of a farmer and his daughter, him holding a hay fork. In the film, Riff Raff and Magenta appear dressed as a farm couple outside a church during the song 'Dammit, Janet!'. We built that set on the drive at Bray, including a huge billboard. Later on a fan asked if they could have the billboard to display in their small town in the USA. There was obviously no problem with that as most of the sets go into the skip at the end of the shoot anyway.

When *Rocky* finished, the 20th Century Fox representative Timothy Burrell asked me to work on another film called *Sky Riders*.

DRAUGHTSMAN
AND ART DIRECTOR

SKY RIDERS

THE DEEP

THE MEDUSA TOUCH

DEATH ON THE NILE

ARABIAN ADVENTURE

Sky Riders

Sky Riders (1976) starred James Coburn, Susannah York, Robert Culp and Charles Aznavour. As art director my first job was to find a monastery, fairly inaccessible, somewhere in Europe. I'd started by searching through masses of books for a suitable location when I had a call from the head office in Los Angeles to say that they had something like $20 million that had been locked up in Greece but was now released, so I should try to find something there.

Off I went to a bookshop in Tottenham Court Road called The Greek Book Shop (who knew!) and I picked up a book called *This is Greece*. According to the book there was a monastery in the middle of the country that looked just right, in a place called Meteora. I learned that the Meteora is a rock formation in central Greece on the edge of the Plain of Thessaly, and this Eastern Orthodox monastery, one of the largest and second only in importance to Mount Athos, is perched right on top – exactly what the script required!

When the day came to show the director, Douglas Hickox, what I had found, Timothy Burrill helped me set up my research, with books and maps from all over Europe, in the 20th Century Fox offices in Soho Square. Once it was set up he went to fetch the director and I heard Douglas say outside the door, 'Well, what has this boy done before?' I didn't hear Timothy's reply but when he walked in with the director and saw the *This is Greece* book (which I still have to this day) and the information on the monastery, he said that his mind was made up and I had to go to Greece immediately and check out the monastery in person.

I was on the 9.30 a.m. flight to Athens the next morning and was met by my Greek interpreter. When I got to the location after seven hours on the road, I was blown away. It seemed to be perfect as there were four monasteries to choose from. While I was there I got a call from Timothy, who was in the USA with the director, to ask if the location was viable. I immediately said 'yes' and Timothy said that they would come over and meet me with hang-gliding experts to see if, from their point of view, it was suitable.

I stayed put until they arrived by helicopter, along with executive producer Sandy Howard. The first to alight was the director and he

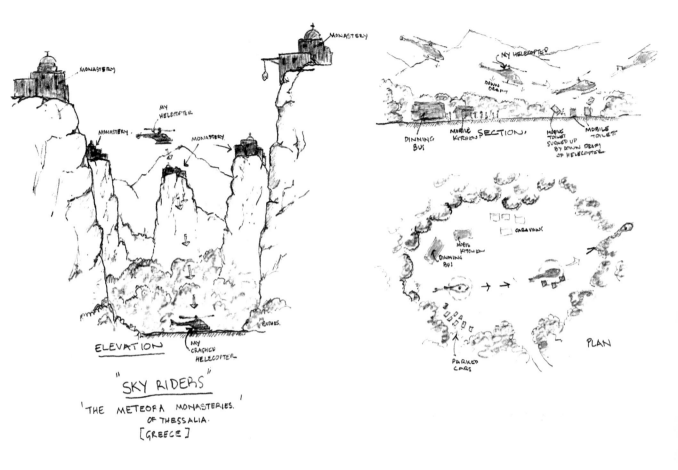

MONASTERY

MONASTERY

MONASTERY
MY
HELICOPTER

MONASTERY

MONASTERY

ELEVATION

MY
CRASHED
HELICOPTER

BUSHES.

"SKY RIDERS"
'THE METEORA MONASTERIES.
OF THESSALIA.
[GREECE]

MY HELICOPTER

DOWN
DRAFT

SECTION.

DINNING
BUS

MOBILE
KITCHEN

MOBILE
TOILET
SUCKED UP
BY DOWN DRAFT
OF HELECOPTER

MOBILE
TOILET

CARAVANS

MOBILE
KITCHEN

DINNING
BUS

PLAN

PARKED
CARS

Diagram of the monastery and surrounding area for *Sky Riders*.

waved me into the helicopter so that I could show him the location. I'd never been in a helicopter before and I'd only seen the monastery from the ground, so I hoped it looked OK. We flew around for about an hour, then they went to lunch. I had a meeting with Douglas later and he said that the location didn't quite work for him. Timothy took me to one side and said that the location was ideal but now I had to go and sell it properly to Douglas.

I asked Douglas why it didn't work and he said that the location looked really good but he didn't see how we could shoot scenes within the monastery. I agreed that aspect would be difficult but said that we could build the interior as a set in the studio in Athens. He said that I couldn't possibly reproduce the interiors accurately on a built set, but how wrong he was! When we did build the set in the studio he had to agree that it was perfect. We had a little help from the stunt coordinator, Peter Brayham, who convinced the director to stay another day and see the location from the road. They were gone for about two hours and when they got back from their recce the director said, 'This is the location.' Then they all left, although I stayed there for four months.

One day, again in the helicopter, we had finished searching for another location and decided that it was time for lunch. Our course took us over our hotel, which had a lovely swimming pool, but I fear that we were a little too low for comfort. The downdraft from the helicopter sucked up all the lilos and sunbeds so the pilot said, 'Perhaps we shouldn't lunch at the hotel today. Let's go and eat with the unit!', who were working on a plateau up in the mountains. I agreed but mentioned that we might be too late for crew catering. 'No, no,' he said. 'It'll only take us five minutes to get there,' so off we went.

When we flew over the unit area, we could see that lunch was still being served. Again we were possibly a little too low and once again the downdraft started to cause havoc with the site, particularly the row of small chemical toilets that were in the line of fire. Unfortunately, one of the toilets was in use and the suction lifted it completely off the ground, leaving the occupant sitting there in full view. In a flash, we decided that maybe lunch wasn't a good idea and flew off looking for more locations. I found myself flying many hours in helicopters over the years. It's absolutely the best way to find tricky locations!

The Deep

The Deep (1977), starring Jacqueline Bisset, Nick Nolte and Robert Shaw, was a whole new adventure for me. I had a call from production designer Tony Masters, who was in LA at the time. When he asked me if I could dive, I thought that he meant high dive in the swimming pool but no - proper underwater diving was required. I was to be the underwater art director, so I'd better learn fast.

I knew someone who had done scuba diving and he put me in touch with a club in Slough. I asked how long it would take to get a Class 3 diving certificate. Apparently it usually took three years but

Diagram of the underwater tank we used in *The Deep*. It was first filled with sea water as there were fish used as background in the scene. Then the tank was drained and refilled with clear water for the actual filming.

if you could hire the pool it would only take a month. It was a bit too expensive for me so I had to call Tony Masters to say I couldn't do the film after all. He got back to me after he had spoken to the producer, Peter Guber, to say that they would pay for the training and the pool hire, so I became a Class 3 diver in double-quick time!

We filmed on location in the Virgin Islands, using an existing shipwreck that had broken into three pieces over the years. In order that the divers, both actors and stunt people, could dive directly onto whichever section of the wreck was needed, the dive boat had to be winched to the relevant areas by cables attached to static buoys. This made it much easier for the underwater camera crew to get the best shots.

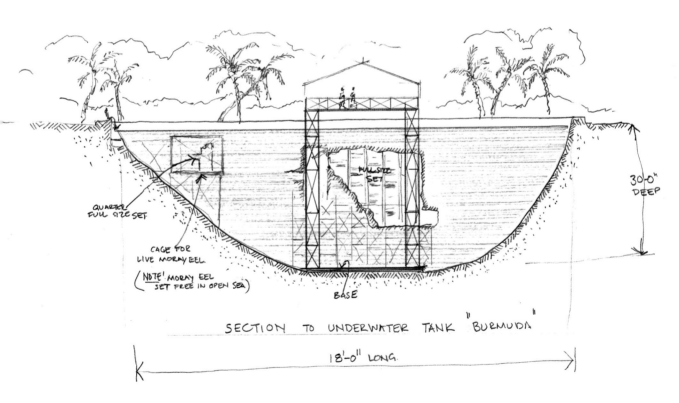

`THE DEEP`

QUARTER FULL SIZE SET

CAGE FOR LIVE MORAY EEL.

(NOTE! MORAY EEL SET FREE IN OPEN SEA)

FULL SIZE SET

BASE

30'-0" DEEP

SECTION TO UNDERWATER TANK "BERMUDA"

18'-0" LONG.

THE ART OF FILM 61

It was an incredible experience. The wreck was 90ft deep at the bow and 30ft deep at the stern. The name of the actual ship was SS *Rohn* and, when it sank, it had sadly lost all 370 souls on board.

I had to dive on the stern as we were going to reproduce that section in the purpose-built tank in Bermuda, where a lot of the action with our stars was to be filmed. The tank was 108ft long, 80ft wide and 30ft deep. Using the tank made the job easier as we could shoot all day, while diving on the wreck would have required the divers to take frequent breaks.

The tank had to be sprayed with polyurethane, which unfortunately was honey-coloured and didn't look like the sea at 60ft down, so we had to paint it blue. However, as you go deeper into the ocean, the colour changes. Matching the colour of the water was very tricky. To do this I painted a piece of metal (we tried it on wooden board but it kept floating to the surface) in strips of different shades of blue and dived down so we could see when the correct colour 'disappeared' at the required depth.

When I was diving on the stern of the wreck I encountered large shoals of fish, which parted as I approached them. It was an amazing experience. There were so many different types of fish – sergeant major, angelfish, parrotfish, cowfish, pufferfish – although I'm no David Attenborough so I couldn't identify them all! There were also many different types of coral, which show up best in torchlight, and many sharks. They were mostly nurse sharks, which aren't dangerous, but I'd seen *Jaws* so I was extremely wary.

I was down with a dive master one day and he showed me an Atlantic goliath grouper. It was the size of a VW Volkswagen and, gosh, it was ugly! The dive master also took me to an area of white coral sand and tapped the sand with his flipper, and a manta ray lifted itself off the ocean floor. I swear it was about 10ft across. That was a sight I'll never forget. It was so graceful.

The dive masters I was with were from the USA: Al Giddins and Stan Waterman. Al's day job was taking photographs for National Geographic and so I felt very safe diving with them both.

For a sequence where the three main actors were supposedly diving on the wreck (but which was filmed in the underwater tank in Bermuda) we had to stage an explosion. After all, it was supposed to

Doing my dream job – an underwater recce on the wreck in the Caribbean!

be a sunken Second World War ammunition ship! For an explosion, total cooperation between the special physical effects team and the director is essential.

Storyboards are key in a situation like this as absolutely everyone has to know in advance exactly what the director wants, so everyone can see where the action is going. The storyboards showed a shot of the ship on the edge of an abyss. This would be a model shot using a 10ft-long miniature in the tank. The model was used because if the scene had been shot in the sea using the actual wreck the camera would have had to be 200ft away and the visibility at that depth is only around 70ft, so that would have made the shot impossible.

In the scene two divers were to be seen escaping from the wreck. This was done optically and I got to operate one of the cameras, which was great fun!

On yet another sequence there was a shark attack on Robert Shaw, where the shark was supposed to bite through his air line. I was in that tank with the shark. I was on one side of the tank with a props man, moving the shark across to the other side for two special effects people to catch with the air line between us. As soon as the shark had the air line in its mouth another special effects man let the air out so a cascade of bubbles went up to the surface.

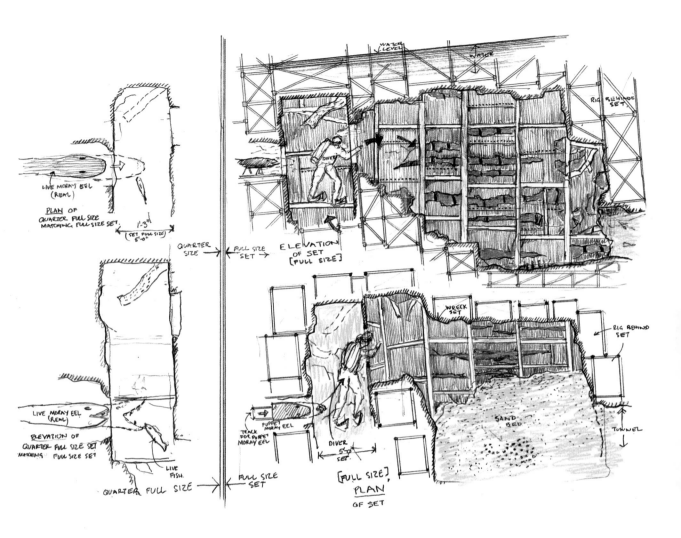

Labels on diagram:
WATER LEVEL
WATER
RIG BEHIND SET
DIVER
ELEVATION OF SET [FULL SIZE]

LIVE MORAY EEL (REAL)
PLAN OF QUARTER FULL SIZE MATCHING FULL SIZE SET
1'-3"
[SET FULL SIZE 5'-0"]
QUARTER SIZE
FULL SIZE SET

LIVE MORAY EEL (REAL)
ELEVATION OF QUARTER FULL SIZE SET MATCHING FULL SIZE SET
LIVE FISH
QUARTER FULL SIZE
FULL SIZE SET

WRECK SET
RIG BEHIND SET
SAND BED
TUNNEL
TRACK FOR PUPPET MORAY EEL
PUPPET MORAY EEL
DIVER 5'-0" SET
[FULL SIZE] PLAN OF SET

Diagram showing how we managed another scene that had a marine costar – this time a moray eel. This is also how we worked with the shark.

I must stress that the shark wasn't injured in any way. We had a marine biologist on hand to advise us on how to handle it properly and the shark was slightly anaesthetised to make the sequence easier to manage. Once the sequence was done the shark was released safely back into the open sea.

I was sent to the laboratory in New York to check that the rushes of the model shot had worked OK. It was only when I was on the plane that I realised I wasn't quite sure exactly what I was looking for – scratch damage on the film, out of focus, bad lighting? If I'd been a cameraman or an editor I would have known exactly what to look for but it looked fine to me. It just goes to show that you really do have to know a little bit about all the jobs in film!

We also had some fake artifacts made to look like solid gold in London, which had been transported to New York and were waiting for collection. I had to personally escort them from New York back to base but was told I couldn't take them as hand luggage. They had to go in the hold so the inevitable happened and they went astray in the airport. I had to stay overnight until they were located and delivered to the hotel. Underwater art director to rushes checker to courier – that's all part of the job!

The Medusa Touch

On *The Medusa Touch* (1978) I was a draughtsman working for art director Peter Mullins. Filmed in Bristol, the movie starred Richard Burton and was about a telekinetic author who caused disasters just by thinking about them.

Sketch of how we wanted the cracked buttresses to look.

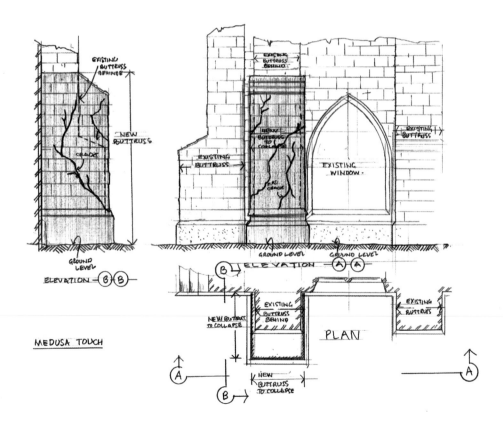

In one scene a church was supposed to collapse. We used polystyrene blocks painted to match the church walls to build the fake buttresses and I used gaffer tape on the blocks, cut into strips to look like cracks. I was quite proud of myself for that. It was all held up by wire and a couple of nails, so when we pulled the wire, down came the buttresses. I'm sure it should have been a special effects job but we did it all ourselves 'on the hoof'. It all looked very realistic.

The finished job, all done with strips of gaffer tape!

Death on the Nile

For the 1978 film *Death on the Nile*, I was art director along with my brother Brian, working for designer Peter Murton with director John Guillermin. When I was asked to work on the film by Peter Murton and read the cast list – David Niven, Peter Ustinov, Maggie Smith, Simon MacCorkindale, Angela Lansbury, George Kennedy, Mia Farrow and Bette Davis – I thought, what a cast! However, I'd previously worked on a film that starred Bette Davis (*The Anniversary*) and on that film the production had found her very difficult to manage, so I warned Peter that she was quite demanding.

One day when I was with Peter in his office in Pinewood, I took a call from the second assistant to say that Peter had been summoned to see Bette Davis on the set on B Stage. Obviously Peter remembered what I'd told him previously so he sent me instead to try to sort out any problems.

'But, but,' I said, 'she asked for you.'

'No, just tell her I had to go on a recce so can't see her.'

Off I went expecting all kinds of trouble. The second assistant had already told me I had to address her as 'Miss Davis'. I asked her if there was a problem with the set, if anything was amiss.

She was filming the scene in the bedroom where her assistant, played by Maggie Smith, was combing her hair. I asked in an extremely polite tone, 'Miss Davis, do you have a problem?' She asked if I was Peter Murton and I replied that he was currently unavailable as he was out on a recce. Her unexpected reply was, 'Well, I just wanted to tell him what a wonderful set this is, probably the best set I've ever filmed on!' Coming from Bette Davis, that was a huge compliment. Of course, I didn't tell Peter the good news straight away, but enjoyed going back to his office and watching his face turn pale as I said, 'Dear oh dear', shaking my head to make him feel bad a little longer. Then I told him that she thought it was a fantastic set and she only wanted to congratulate him. Off he went like a shot to claim the praise, obviously back from the recce a lot sooner than expected!

I spent a lot of time on *Death on the Nile* with the cast and crew. The director was a little tricky to deal with but very good at his job. Being the only art director on location, I had to solve any problems that cropped up on the spot. In those days there was no such thing as a mobile phone and, as it took up to three weeks to book a call to the UK, there was no one to turn to for help, so I really had to think on my feet!

Director John Guillermin and director of photography Jack Cardiff having a serious conversation on the boat.

My first visit on arriving in Cairo was to the Great Pyramids at Giza with Peter Murton, who said that we had to climb to the top. I think they're around 400ft high, so I was terrified! The reason for all this exertion was a scene in the film where the action takes place at the top of the pyramid. I guess these days we wouldn't be allowed to do this for Health-and-Safety reasons, but would have to build it as a set instead. During the descent I wore the seat of my trousers out as the blocks of stone are very large and a bit sharp, and I had to sit and slide a bit on every stone until I reached the bottom. I breathed a big sigh of relief to feel the ground under my feet!

Sketch of the Aswan location.

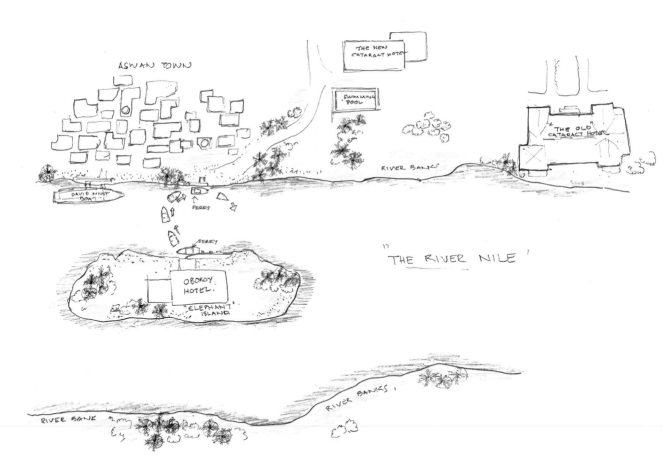

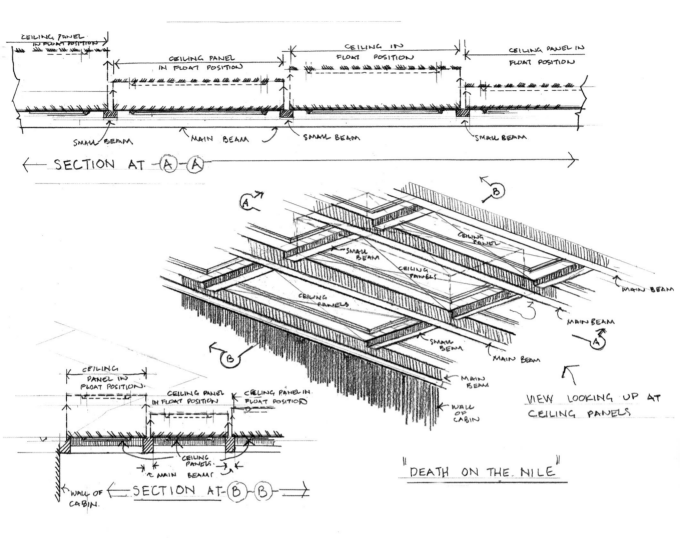

SECTION AT (A) (A)

CEILING PANEL IN FLOAT POSITION

CEILING PANEL IN FLOAT POSITION

CEILING IN FLOAT POSITION

CEILING PANEL IN FLOAT POSITION

SMALL BEAM

MAIN BEAM

SMALL BEAM

SMALL BEAM

VIEW LOOKING UP AT CEILING PANELS

"DEATH ON THE NILE"

SECTION AT (B) (B)

CEILING PANEL IN FLOAT POSITION.

CEILING PANEL IN FLOAT POSITION

CEILING PANEL IN FLOAT POSITION

CEILING PANELS.

MAIN BEAM

WALL OF CABIN.

Diagram of the interior of SS *Karnak*.

One of my first jobs in Egypt was to survey the boat we were going to use, which was the historic ship SS *Memnon*, renamed SS *Karnak* for the film. We had to fit cladding to suit the design of the film. I had to measure everything precisely because the cladding was going to be built in one piece back in Pinewood. I wasn't involved in the build but in order for them to be able to transport the cladding – so they knew it would fit in the aeroplane – they had to build a mock-up aircraft cargo hold in the studio. Luckily it all fitted well and was safely delivered. The art department also had to build a mock-up of the entire boat for a night shoot on one of the stages, which was flooded with 4in of water. Even I couldn't tell which one was which when I saw it on the screen!

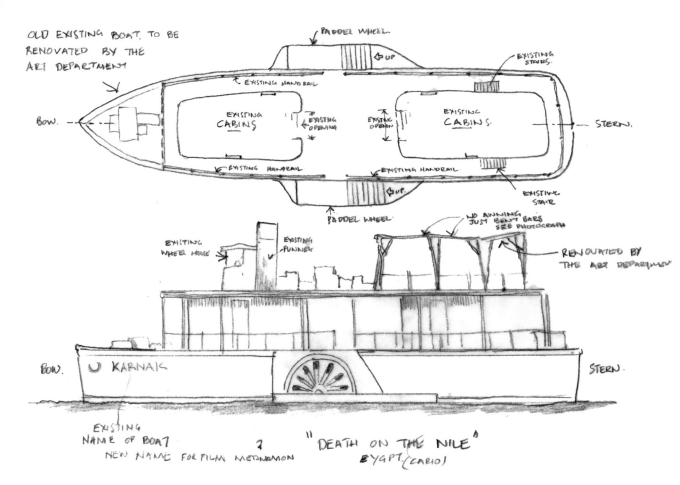

OLD EXISTING BOAT. TO BE
RENOVATED BY THE
ART DEPARTMENT

PADDEL WHEEL

EXISTING STAIRS.

BOW.

EXISTING HANDRAIL

EXISTING
CABINS

EXISTING
OPENING

EXISTING
OPENING

EXISTING
CABINS.

STERN.

EXISTING HANDRAIL

EXISTING HANDRAIL

EXISTING
STAIR

UP

PADDEL WHEEL

NO AWNING
JUST BENT BARS
SEE PHOTOGRAPH

EXISTING
WHEEL HOUSE

EXISTING
FUNNEL

RENOVATED BY
THE ART DEPARTMENT

BOW.

KARNAIK

STERN.

EXISTING
NAME OF BOAT?

NEW NAME FOR FILM MEDNAMON

?

"DEATH ON THE NILE"
EYGPT. (CARIO)

Diagram showing a side
view of the boat.

A nice snap of me
lounging on the rear deck
of the boat.

Looking out from the hotel balcony over the gardens, which we had to dress out with 'greens'.

Checking out a water-wheel for background information.

We had to build a large sphinx-like head on the banks of the Nile, which was about 40ft high. It was very hot, about 45°C, when we started the build. The metal scaffold tubes were far too hot to handle so we had to change plans and build the structure with wood. The construction manager had made a small model of the head back at Pinewood, which I carried with me but, as ever, customs in Egypt had to have it opened as they thought it might be a contraband artefact. It was screwed down so tight and, of course, no one had a screwdriver, but we managed and all was OK in the end.

One of the many problems I had was the director wanting a sign on a door on the boat to say 'WC' or 'toilet' or whatever to match the period. I decided that I would visit an old hotel, which was from the same period as the boat, and have a look to see if I could find something suitable.

The hotel was on the mainland in Aswan and my office was on Elephantine Island, so the only way to the mainland was by ferry. Sitting next to me on the ferry was David Niven. He was going to meet up with his son who, by chance, was on a cruise liner docked in Aswan. He asked what I was doing so I told him and, knowing that the director was a bit of a stickler, he wished me the best of luck!

The old Cataract Hotel, which was lovely but didn't give me the inspiration I needed for the door sign!

Needless to say, I failed. I couldn't find a suitable sign anywhere, so I decided to go back to my hotel and make one myself. On my return trip, who should be there again but David Niven! When he found out I'd had no luck he offered to help but I declined – after all, he was the star of the show, not my assistant!

When the next morning came, I was a bit nervous that the sign wasn't exactly what John Guillermin wanted. I was just about to show it to him when David Niven and Peter Ustinov arrived on the boat for a rehearsal. Having spotted me and realising what was about to happen, David shouted, 'John, John, I seem to have forgotten my script!' Of course he hadn't, as I realised when he winked at me, but it was a very welcome distraction. So John looked at the sign briefly, said it was discreet and OK, and rushed off to sort out the much more important problem of David and his lines! What a true gentleman David Niven was.

Another challenge I had, amongst many, was having to paint a felucca – a traditional Egyptian wooden sailing boat – the same shade of blue as SS *Memnon*. I was up all night with a painter doing the job but, because we had to use what was at hand, it wasn't quite the same colour. When the cast and crew left the boat, the director asked me to join him. I thought he'd noticed that the colour was different so I explained that the particular shade of the paintwork was because of the strong sunlight on the new paint, which made it look slightly purple, so there wasn't a lot that I could do about it. Pointing to a BOAC aircraft in the sky overhead, I said that if he wasn't satisfied with my work, I'd be on that flight tomorrow back to London, as I just couldn't take much more!

Later the producer, Richard Goodwin, called me into his office and I thought, *This is it, I'm going home!* But surprisingly, he said that John was impressed with me taking full responsibility and he wanted me to stay on the film. It just shows that honesty is the best policy!

I was staying in Shepheard's Hotel in Cairo. Originally called Hotel des Anglais, it was renamed after its founder, Samuel Shepheard. It was one of the most celebrated hotels in the world from the middle of the nineteenth century until it burned down in 1952, with the new version being built soon after that.

At the time I was working with a line producer who was quite well known and influential in Egypt. When the aircraft with all our equipment landed at the airport, it was quickly surrounded by armed guards. It transpired that money, around 14,000 Egyptian pounds, had to change hands before the equipment would be released. That was a new one for me but the line producer was very familiar with the procedure! He was called away, which meant he had to leave me in charge of the money, with instructions to discreetly give it to whoever approached me for it. He promised to have a packed lunch sent to me. The lunch arrived in a box wrapped with a pink ribbon: champagne and smoked salmon sandwiche – very posh!

This is when it started to get a bit cloak and dagger. The fixer, called Dimitri, arrived and said we should go to the gents' toilets. I thought that sounded a bit dodgy but went along with it. The money changed hands and he told me to wait five minutes after he left so we wouldn't be seen leaving the gents' together. By the time I got to where I could see the aircraft, the armed guards were already getting into their vehicles and leaving, so we were then free to unload the plane.

This line producer was even more influential than I imagined. I mentioned to him that I would like to call my wife and family but that it took so long to get a call booked. However, he had a connection at the palace, which was President Nasser's home at the time, so along we went into an office in the palace. I was able to call my wife immediately, and she promptly asked why it had taken me so long to call her. Some people are never pleased!

Arabian Adventure

Working on this film, *Arabian Adventure*, was quite an experience! I agreed to work on the film because Elliot Scott and Reg Bream were old friends. Elliot had a reputation for producing inexpensive designs that looked amazing. He always managed to incorporate stock items of old sets into his new designs. Steven Spielberg used to call him 'Grandad' and thought the world of him.

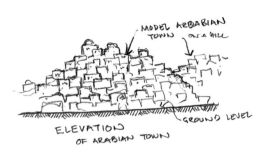

"ARABIAN ADVENTURE"

MODEL ARABIAN TOWN ON A HILL

ELEVATION OF ARABIAN TOWN

GROUND LEVEL

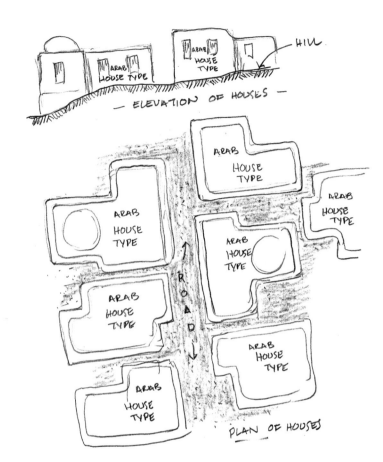

HILL

— ELEVATION OF HOUSES —

ARAB HOUSE TYPE

ARAB HOUSE TYPE

ARAB HOUSE TYPE

ARAB HOUSE TYPE

ARAB HOUSE TYPE

ARAB HOUSE TYPE

ARAB HOUSE TYPE

ROAD

PLAN OF HOUSES

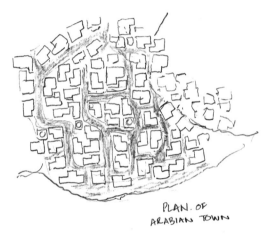

PLAN. OF ARABIAN TOWN

Diagram of the model Arabian town we had to construct.

We had to build a model of an Arabian town on a hill. Elliot's idea was to make about five different types of houses at scale and set them up on the hills. The houses were moulds and we set them up at random, creating the idea of streets. There was no real drawing involved, just set dressing, but it was very effective.

Elliot was the first art director that I had worked for when I started and I had the good fortune to work on many subsequent films with him. I learned so much from him and draughtsman Reg Bream. In this job you never stop learning; each new project brings a different challenge.

ART DIRECTOR

SUPERMAN II
THE DARK CRYSTAL
THE GREAT MUPPET CAPER

Superman II

Superman II (1980), starring Christopher Reeve, was filmed at Pinewood Studios with director Richard Lester, designer Peter Murton, construction manager Terry Apsey and set decorator Peter Young. Unfortunately, during this time I was going through a divorce, which was a very unhappy time for me, but both Peter Young and Peter Murton were very kind and saw me through the worst of it.

We designed and built a full New York street set on the back lot. It took around four months to construct. Peter Young, a master of his craft, did an excellent job with his product placement, getting as many companies as possible to offer their goods at no cost for set dressing or to be worn or driven by the actors. It was good value for the production and good advertising for the companies!

Once, when Peter Young was struggling to dress a mannequin in designer underwear, he was so engrossed in trying to pull on the knickers that he wasn't aware that Richard Lester and the crew had all downed tools and were watching him. They gave him a round of applause when he finally finished the job – much to his embarrassment! It was a great crew and a lot of fun was had by all throughout the shoot.

Me with director Richard Lester and producer Alexander Salkind.

The *Superman II* street under construction.

Me on the finished set.

The ability to thoroughly research a subject is vital in designing and constructing any film set as audiences are very discerning and it can spoil their enjoyment if everything doesn't look absolutely right for the style of film. In this instance I went to a mid-American town and took reels of photographs and made many sketches. You can look all this up the easy way but there's no substitute for a proper recce. The street furniture – signs, telephone booths, streetlamps, as well as vehicles – all had to be authentic for the period. The telephone booths were rigged so that they collapsed, as in the story, the Elders (led by Terence Stamp as General Zod) blew the street furniture down the street. This was all set up in conjunction with the special physical effects crew – a lot of planning involved!

Naturally, in a film like this, there were lots of action shots, and this is where a comprehensive storyboard comes in handy. Storyboards are an extremely helpful tool when it comes to planning an action scene where special physical effects will be used. The storyboard artist works very closely with the director to translate sequences from the script into a series of illustrations in order to show precisely what the director wants to achieve, so that the heads of department who will be involved in the sequence know exactly what is required. This saves the production a lot of time and one or two arguments.

On the street set, there was another scene involving an accident at the crossroads, caused by Zod using his heat vision to blow up cars and making a tanker glow red-hot. Superman cools it down by blowing on the tanker and uses the tanker's mirror to deflect Zod's vision, thus stopping the explosions. Further on in the sequence a bus full of passengers comes into view and one of the Elders lifts the bus and starts to throw it towards a parked van, again saved by Superman.

The problem here was, how were we going to achieve this shot with the bus? Obviously, the special physical effects team had all the answers! They used a crane to lift the bus, complete with passengers, towards Superman. The bus travelled with Superman into the parked van, which collapsed and crumbled. The van was made out of soft metal that fell apart on impact. The shot was very effective.

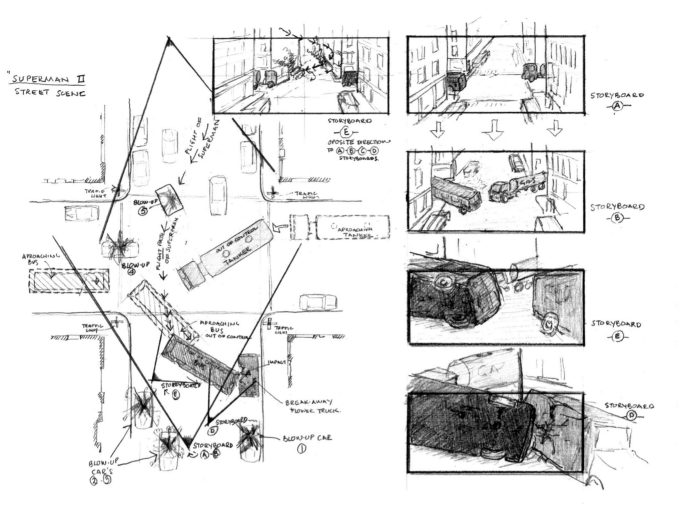

Diagram of the bus crash sequence.

In the same scene Superman gets involved in a fight with Zod, who jumps on Superman and drives a hole into the road. To do this we built a small section of the road on a stage, about 12ft up, with a camouflaged hole in it, which allowed the stuntmen recreating the fight to effectively disappear. The section of the road looked so plausible that one of the painters who was putting the finishing touches to the set stepped back to admire his work, slipped into the 'hole' and disappeared. We knew then it would work just fine!

There was another sequence in the film in which Superman fights the Elders amongst the skyscrapers. In one shot the hero hits one of the Elders and throws him out of an office window.

This was a little tricky to put together, so take a look at the diagram opposite and you'll see how we achieved this sequence - much easier than trying to explain. The set was built as normal, but we then hinged it so that it could turn almost upside down.

The crash sequence starting.

The crash sequence with a taxi being crushed by a lamppost, showing rigging.

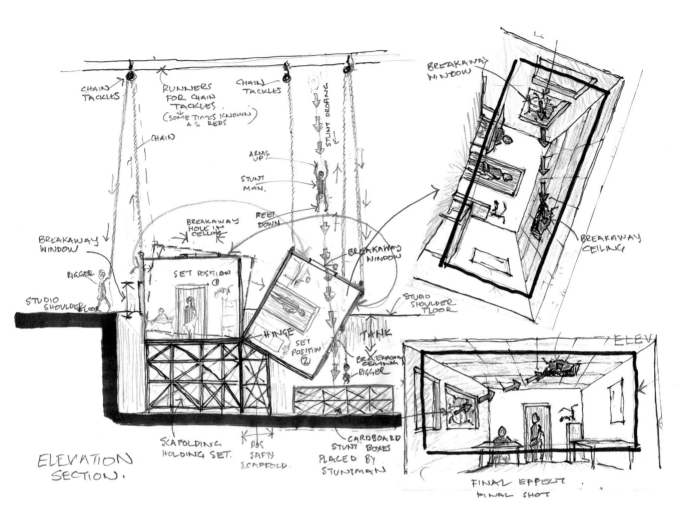

Inside the diagram, the following labels appear:

CHAIN TACKLES · RUNNERS FOR CHAIN TACKLES (SOME TIMES KNOWN AS REDS) · CHAIN TACKLES · BREAKAWAY WINDOW · CHAIN · STUNT DROPNS · ARMS UP! · STUNT MAN · FEET DOWN · BREAKAWAY HOLE IN CEILING · BREAKAWAY WINDOW · SET POSITION ① · BREAKAWAY WINDOW · BREAKAWAY CEILING · STUDIO SHOULDER FLOOR · HINGE · SET POSITION ② · STUDIO SHOULDER FLOOR · TANK · BREAKAWAY CEILING · RIGGER · BREAKAWAY WINDOW · RIGGER · STUDIO SHOULDER FLOOR · ELEV · SCAFFOLDING HOLDING SET. · POS SAFTY SCAFFOLD. · CARDBOARD STUNT BOXES PLACED BY STUNTMAN · FINAL EFFECT FINAL SHOT

ELEVATION SECTION.

Diagram of how we set up the special effects set with Superman fighting the Elders.

Inside the office a model of a secretary was sitting typing. I'd thought of everything: the paper in the typewriter was stiffened, her pearls were stuck to her neck so they wouldn't fall off, and her hair was starched so it wouldn't move when she went upside down. I assumed all was OK. However, when Richard saw the rushes the following day, he said that it didn't work – when the set moved, she looked odd. Apparently her breasts were too high up, too close to her neck. How on earth was I supposed to fix that? We used the shot anyway, so you might spot her and see what you think if you see the film again.

Another difficult shot was where Superman had a fight in a bar. Just like in a western film, he punched the Elder through the saloon door out onto the walkway. A truck was parked outside, loaded with chickens that would fly in all directions when we let them loose. It should have been melons but, because of gravity, we couldn't get them to fall in the right way.

We shot the sequences of the ice palace on the 007 Stage at Pinewood. It was built from polystyrene and stretched polythene and it had to match the original set built by John Barry for *Superman*. This was where the kryptonite – a green shard of glass in the centre – was stored. Legend has it that John Barry had seen a piece of crystal rock in a book and this was where the idea came from.

Drawing of how we managed to create the chicken sequence.

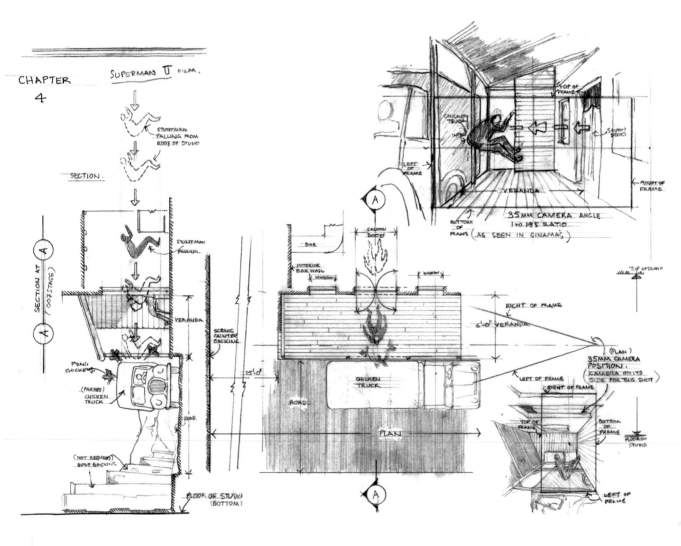

We had rails set up in the roof of the stage holding the bogie for the wires, which were used to give the illusion of Superman flying. The whole of this sequence was worked out in the art department with cardboard models and storyboards. We were definitely boys with toys!

The Niagara Falls sequence, shot on location, needed very careful planning by us in conjunction with the special physical effects unit. One of the really exciting things I did was to change the colour of the Falls using something called a 'lighting hut', which projected the coloured lights onto the water – red, white and blue. I thoroughly enjoyed doing that and it was a real winner.

For another scene Richard Lester wanted Lois Lane and Superman to have a picnic in a corn field with corn silos in the background, so we found a good location in Canada. However, Richard wanted a tree in the shot but there wasn't a tree in sight. Big problem! Driving back to my hotel, I passed a farm that had exactly the right tree. I asked the farmer if we could buy it and he said he'd been meaning to chop it down for years so we were more than welcome to it. We enlisted the help of tree experts who lifted it, complete with roots, to replant it at the location. Everything was going OK until we had to dig the new hole for the tree. The machine that should have dug the hole was part of the vehicle carrying the tree and it couldn't do

Niagara Falls,
extremely chilly!

the two things at once, so we had to find a replacement. This digger
was fairly old and the hydraulics failed, which sent fluid all over
the picnic area. What a drama! Can you imagine trying to clean up
hydraulic fluid from growing corn? It could have been a sequence
from a *Carry On* film! We managed it eventually but this is just the
kind of problem we have to solve on location as we're supposed to
leave everything exactly the same as we found it, if not better.

For another sequence on location in Canada we had to reproduce
a fire on a bridge carrying a pipeline to an oil refinery. Obviously we
couldn't set a fire close to the real refinery – that would be far too
dangerous even for a film crew – so we built a set that we could
burn with the actual refinery in the background, at least a mile away.
We could only shoot the sequence when the wind was in the right
direction, away from the refinery. We did our best to position the
bridge with the prevailing wind coming towards the set. Happily
Superman came to the rescue and put the fire out and the world
was saved yet again!

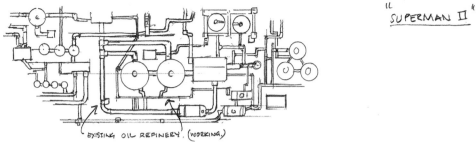

"SUPERMAN II"

EXISTING OIL REFINERY. (WORKING.)

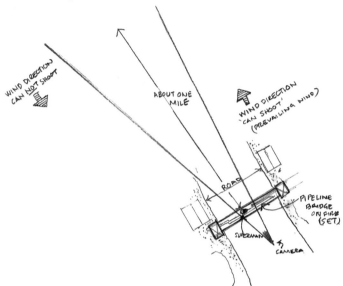

WIND DIRECTION CAN NOT SHOOT

ABOUT ONE MILE

WIND DIRECTION 'CAN SHOOT' (PREVAILING WIND)

ROAD

PIPELINE BRIDGE ON FIRE (SET)

SUPERMAN

CAMERA

Sketch showing how we managed to film the exploding oil refinery without causing any damage.

The oil refinery 'gantry' on fire.

As I might have mentioned, I love a helicopter ride, so flying over the Rocky Mountains at 12,000ft looking for another location was a pure delight. On the way back I asked the pilot if he would fly over my apartment, which he did. My girlfriend from the UK (now my wife) was sunbathing on the balcony. She wasn't best pleased as she thought that it was a bit creepy!

Recce on the Rockies, very spectacular.

The Dark Crystal

Working on *The Dark Crystal* (1982) with production designer Harry Lange and my brother Brian as joint art director was a whole new concept! The film used animatronics: very sophisticated mechanical puppets that can be pre-programmed, controlled remotely or moved by a combination of mechanics, electronics and human performers. The sets included a crystal chamber, which had to accommodate both the puppeteers and the animatronic characters. It had to be built on rostrums that were 4ft 6in above the ground so that the humans could operate the creatures out of sight of the camera lens.

The actual dark crystal was an 8ft-tall fibreglass construction. We did try Perspex cut in different shapes to reflect the facets of a crystal but that didn't work very well as the light travels very differently through Perspex and we couldn't get the right effect. The answer we came up with was to treat it like a sculpture, making a cast in fibreglass. The crystal was purple and white and Ossie Morris, the director of photography, and his lighting gaffer John Harman came up with a tricky lighting pattern to make it work on the screen.

Section plan of how we filmed the puppets without exposing the puppeteers.

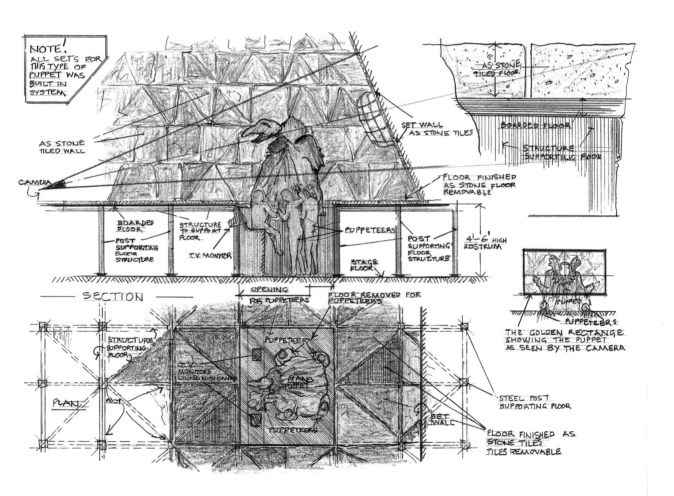

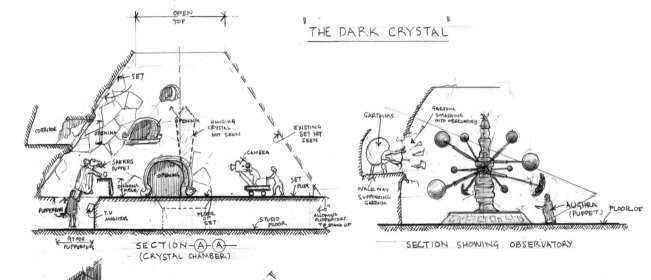

"THE DARK CRYSTAL"

SECTION—A—A
(CRYSTAL CHAMBER)

SECTION SHOWING OBSERVATORY

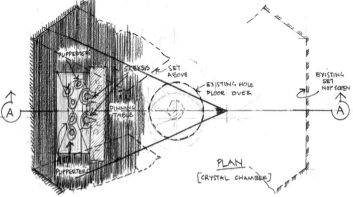

PLAN
[CRYSTAL CHAMBER]

Diagram of the crystal chamber.

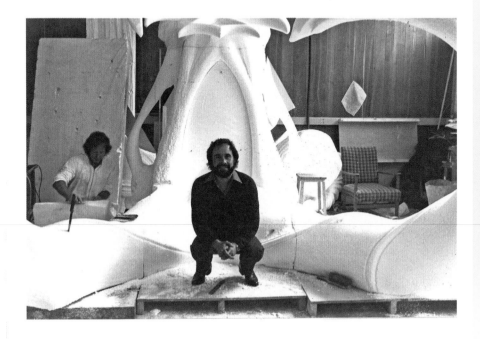

Me with the crystal throne under construction.

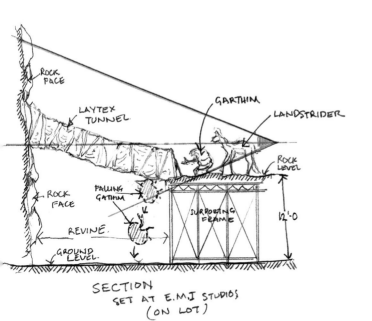

SECTION
SET AT E.M.I STUDIOS
(ON LOT)

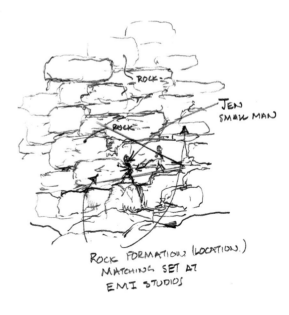

ROCK FORMATION (LOCATION.)
MATCHING SET AT
EMI STUDIOS

Section of the cave set built at EMI Studios (on the left) to match the rock formation in Yorkshire (on the right).

Another set on the back lot of EMI Studios was a ravine between a rock face and a standing rock, where the Garthim (baddies) were attacking Gelflings (goodies) called Jen (Jim Henson) and Kira (Kathryn Mullen).

Before we built the actual set, we constructed a detailed card model so that the director, the cinematographer and I could work out how the scene was going to be shot and make sure we wouldn't hit any snags on the day. In the studio we constructed a latex tunnel connecting the standing rock to the rock face where the Garthims would fall into the ravine. This was matched to the North Yorkshire location (which was looked after by art director Malcolm Stone) where Jen had to scale the rock face. For this sequence and for ease of manipulation, Jim Henson used both puppets and a small actor called Kiran Shah, who doubled for puppet Jen to do the actual climb.

Another challenge was Aughra's orrery. Aughra was a mysterious character who understood both science and spiritual matters. The orrery was hugely complicated, with intricately revolving apparatus to represent the movement of the planets in the solar system, and was constructed by the special effects department.

The orrery under construction.

The completed orrery ready for action.

Jim Henson on set with
the lead Gelfling puppets.

Clockwise from left:
Me with Roy Field, one
of the best special visual
effects cinematographers
in the business; Me and
Jim Henson on location
in Yorkshire; Me and
assistant director Dusty
Symonds on location
in Yorkshire.

The *Dark Crystal* crew on set.

Another favourite set of mine was the interior of the Pod village where the Pod people were merrymaking until the Garthims battered their way in, for which we built a breakaway wall. For some reason I got quite attached to the Pod people even though they were only puppets!

You can imagine that this film was hugely enjoyable to work on, although it tested us all to the limit. But that's why we love our job: every day there's another challenge!

The Great Muppet Caper

When I first started on *The Great Muppet Caper* (1981) I was already involved with **The Dark Crystal**, both films being for Jim Henson and Frank Oz. Puppets have been used since entertainment began, from Punch and Judy, who have terrified and entertained children in equal measure since the seventeenth century, to marionettes operated by strings such as the classic *Thunderbirds*, right through to the almost life-sized characters designed by Jim Henson for *Sesame Street* and *The Muppets,* and then beyond to remote-controlled animatronics.

Muppets cycle ride set-up sketch.

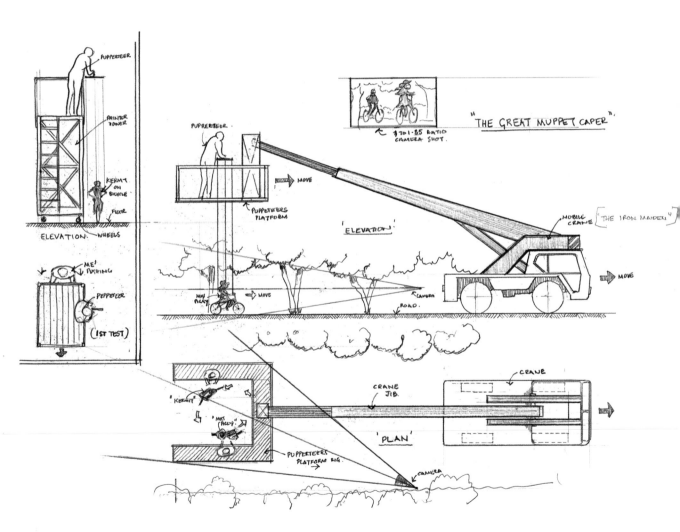

There was a sequence in *The Great Muppet Caper* where Miss Piggy and Kermit had to perform a figure of eight on bicycles to the song 'Couldn't We Ride'. It needed another big rig for the puppeteers to work in, which we fixed to a crane, aptly named the Iron Maiden. However, Jim suggested that in order to make it more mobile we could mount the contraption on a golf cart. I did say that it would be too heavy and topple over but he insisted and so topple over it did. I didn't like to say, 'I told you so!'

After Kermit and Miss Piggy's figure-of-eight scene, the sequence had to include all the puppets riding bicycles, but how could we manage that? Special effects supervisor Brian Smithies suggested that we join the bikes with rods and have them all being towed by someone on a tricycle out of shot, using a thin wire that wouldn't show up. Given that the passengers were puppets, there wasn't a lot of weight involved and it worked very well. The bicycles themselves took a bit of time as they all had to fit the different characters so had to be built from scratch.

Setting up the cycle rig in Battersea.

We had a lot of fun doing a scene with a bus carrying all the puppeteers and the radio-controlled puppets. We built it on a Transit van chassis and it did look good on screen as well as being thoroughly roadworthy.

Opposite: Bicycle
sequence storyboards.

Me testing the rig and
helping Kermit balance on
his bike!

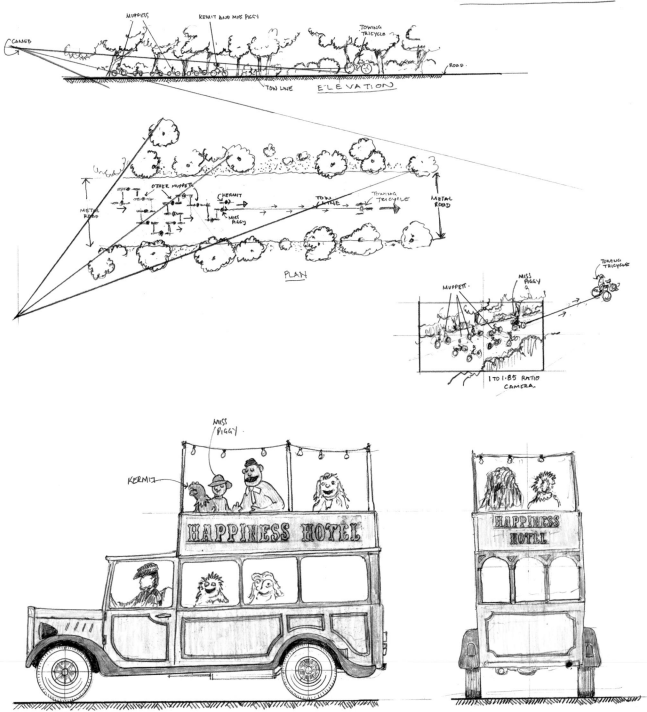

"THE GREAT MUPPET CAPER"

ELEVATION

PLAN

1 TO 1·85 RATIO CAMERA.

HAPPINESS HOTEL

HAPPINESS HOTEL

SIDE VIEW.

REAR VIEW.

The Happiness Hotel was a location in London where we had to have a car, driven by a puppet, go into the hotel through the front door, so the car had to be small enough to fit. For this shot we had to have special permission from the police, who are usually very accommodating to film crews as long as the production selects times for the shoot that don't interfere too much with the general flow of traffic.

One sequence in Albuquerque, New Mexico, involved Animal eating a plaque - similar to the MGM logo but with Animal's face instead of the lion. The plaque came from the UK but wasn't painted, so I got my paint and brushes out and started. However, it was freezing cold, which seems odd in New Mexico, but in the desert areas it gets pretty bad at night. The paint was just about freezing on my brush so I had to find heaters to warm me and the paint up.

Drawing of how we planned the car entering the hotel.

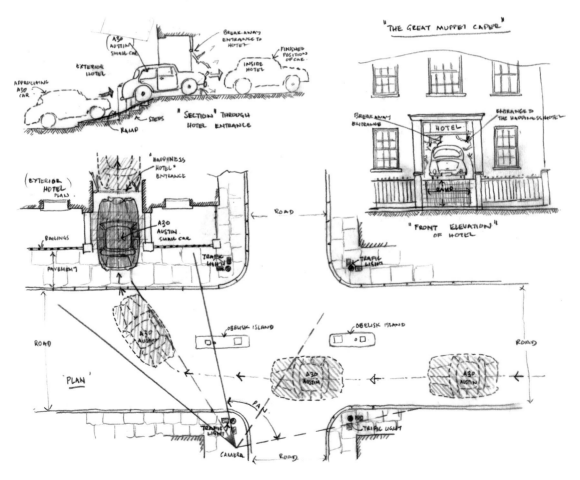

In another scene Fozzie Bear had to fly in a hot-air balloon and crash land in a street in New Mexico, which was a set built on a stage in Elstree Studios. The scene involved live action with cars; painters working on scaffolding; people playing with a basketball, which was thrown up and landed in a paint bucket; and a painter doing a backward somersault onto the ground, all while Fozzie was singing – total mayhem!

The legendary cinematographer Ossie Morris had a problem with the light reflecting on all the car windscreens, so I thought that the easiest option would be to remove them. However, Ossie said, quite rightly, that it would look terrible, so we had to erect a white canvas over the set to deflect the glare. As you can imagine, working with Jim Henson and Frank Oz was always a joy. There was never a dull moment!

Shooting the MGM-style logo in New Mexico.

Opposite: Storyboards showing the action and mayhem caused by Fozzie Bear's balloon landing.

SCENE 2   EXT. SKY - DAY.

FOZZIE YANKS THE RIP CORD . . . .

SCENE 3 - EXT. STREET - DAY.

IT LANDS WITH A WHOOSH ON A STREET IN A
METROPOLITAN CITY . . . .

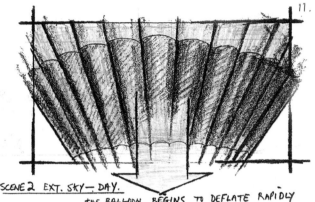

SCENE 2 EXT. SKY - DAY.

. . . . THE BALLOON BEGINS TO DEFLATE RAPIDLY
AND PLUMMETS EARTHWARD.

SCENE 3 - EXT. STREET - DAY.

. . . . COVERED IMMEDIATELY BY THE LARGE DEFLATED
BALLOON.

SCENE 3 EXT. STREET - DAY

AS FOZZIE SINGS " : . . . . . AND ME ! " - BASKETBALL PLAYER
JUMPS AND "SCORES", DROPPING BALL INTO PAINT PAIL

SCENE 3 EXT - STREET.

AS BASKETBALL DROPS INTO PAIL PAINTER DOES
BACKWARD SOMERSAULT FROM CRADLE TO GROUND
FOZZIE SINGS : — "THERE'll BE HEROES BOLD"
               THERE'll BE COMEDY

The Muppets street scene, with the painters on the scaffolding.

The radio-controlled Muppets in the balloon basket.

The crew preparing the hot-air balloon for take-off.

Jim Henson with Fozzie, Gonzo and Kermit.

Just hanging around
waiting for something to
happen in the desert!

Me and the American
camera crew.

ART DIRECTOR AND PRODUCTION DESIGNER

SUPERGIRL
KING DAVID
SPIES LIKE US
LABYRINTH
ALIENS

Supergirl

For *Supergirl* (1984) we built a big set on the back lot at Pinewood Studios, designed by Richard Macdonald with director Jeannot Szwarc. It was about a quarter of a mile long with the appropriate built-in perspective and it was the biggest perspective set I have ever been involved with. The street had to look much longer than the space we had on the back lot so we used cut-out cars, then smaller cars and models of little people in the distance crossing the road. It worked very well.

I had once again been to the USA to recce in the Midwest so that we could create a good replica of an average American town. The signage was particularly important to get right, as well as the traffic lights and gas station. Even the most minute of details have to be correct otherwise someone in the audience is bound to spot the mistakes.

Looking at the card model of the Smallville set with Supergirl actress Helen Slater and production designer Richard Macdonald.

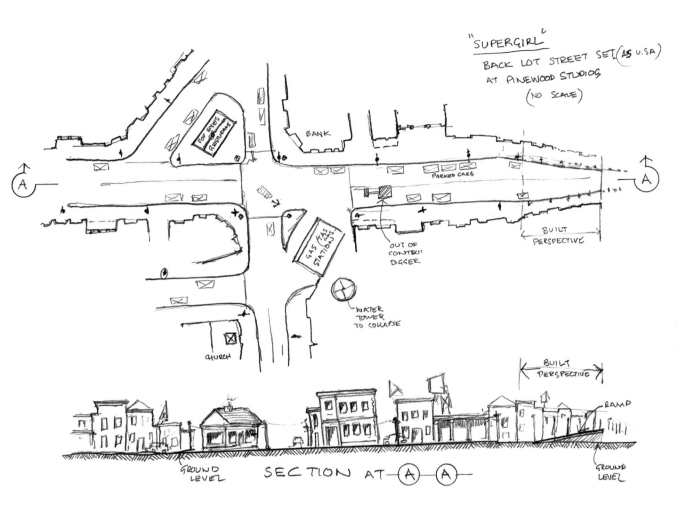

"SUPERGIRL"
BACK LOT STREET SET (AS U.SA)
AT PINEWOOD STUDIOS
(NO SCALE)

BANK

POP EYE'S RESTAURANT

PARKED CARS

BUILT PERSPECTIVE

OUT OF CONTROL DIGGER

GAS STATION

WATER TOWER TO COLLAPSE

CHURCH

BUILT PERSPECTIVE

RAMP

GROUND LEVEL

SECTION AT —Ⓐ Ⓐ—

GROUND LEVEL

Draft sketch of the
Supergirl street section.

One of the sponsors was a fast-food company who wanted their restaurant very visible on the set. There was some dispute about the company's logo, which was very prominent on top of their building. The director hated it and it was taken down for filming but put back when their representative came to check that the restaurant's exterior and interior were both exactly to their specifications. He was pleasantly shocked when he walked onto the set as by this time it was complete with vehicles so he said that he thought he was in America. It was so realistic and he got so engrossed in his job that he walked off the edge of the set. Luckily it wasn't far to fall so there was no harm done, just a red face!

The street set under construction.

The street set partially dressed as the camera would see it.

The *Supergirl* street dressed and ready for action.

Me and designer Richard Macdonald celebrating.

Another sponsor was a prominent fuel company who were a bit more hesitant about their name being on a gas station that was to be blown up for a stunt, so we renamed it. My initials are now immortalised on the big screen as TAS Gas. The stunt involved a remotely controlled runaway digger that crashed into the gas station, setting it alight. This was done under the watchful eye of special effects supervisor John Evans.

Another set was dodgem cars in a fairground, so we had to replace all the bodywork of the UK dodgems so that they looked like American football players' heads. It was really funny at the time!

Peter O'Toole played Zaltar, whose palace was built on the 007 Stage at Pinewood. Supergirl had to travel the length of the set in a huge Perspex ball that was hung from the top of the stage. Between us in the art department, the special effects team and the construction crew we worked it out and it looked really convincing – teamwork!

Me, ever immortalised as TAS Gas. The crane in the middle of the street was used for the Supergirl flying rig and Selena's Rolls-Royce.

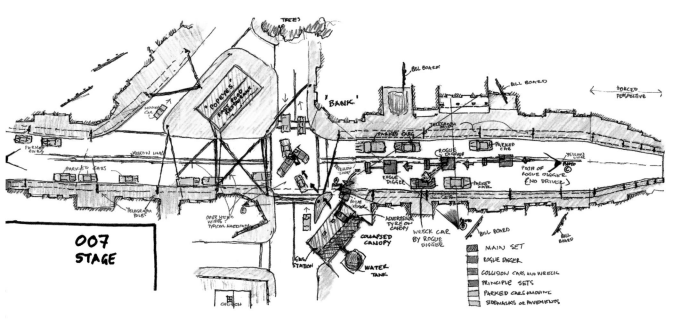

Top: Draft sketch of the crash sequence with all the camera angles. The street had a built-in perspective to give the illusion of length.

Bottom: An aerial shot of the finished set on the back lot at Pinewood.

One of the vehicles used in the crash sequence with (left to right): storyboard artist Mike Ploog, me and concept artist Simon Murton.

A happy crew celebrating on set (left to right): Jeannot Szwarc, me, Richard Macdonald and Mike Ploog.

Left to right: camera operator Freddie Cooper, director of photography Alan Hume, first assistant director Derek Cracknell and me – with Richard Macdonald 'directing' in the background!

Zaltar's Palace under construction.

King David

Ken Adam was the production designer on *King David* (1985). The director Bruce Beresford and director of photography Don McAlpine were both Australian and the film starred Richard Gere as King David. There were a lot of locations in Italy, such as Abruzzo, Sardinia and Rome, as well as built sets at Pinewood Studios. In one of the locations we had to reproduce a wooded area where a chariot chase was to take place. During the action, one of the chariots had to lose a wheel. This action shot had been rehearsed in great detail back in the UK with the special physical effects crew, so it all went smoothly on the location - another example of great teamwork saving time and money.

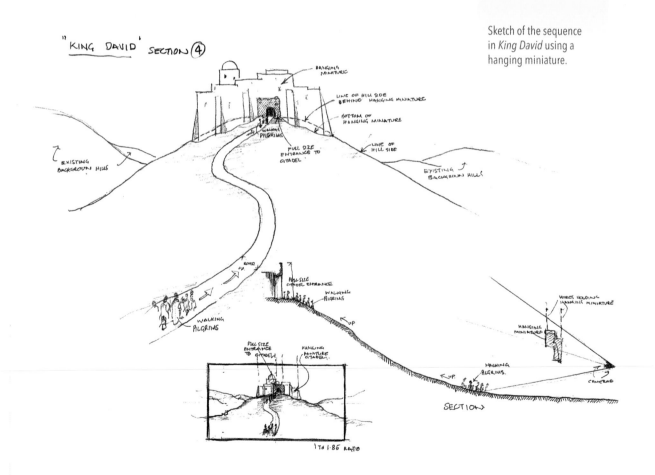

Sketch of the sequence in *King David* using a hanging miniature.

For one sequence we had to use a 'hanging miniature' (see Chapter 9 for more explanation on this). The hills on the location were all hillocks covered with grass but the scene was set in a desert, so we removed all the grass with a bulldozer. As you can see, it's not just sitting at a drawing board in our department. We actually have to get out there and get our hands dirty!

Another day and another location: King David had to climb down a well. The well itself was only 4ft deep but obviously that was only the start of the sequence. The rest of his climb was on a set in Pinewood Studios with simulated moonlight to add atmosphere. Sorry to spoil the illusion!

One of the locations was a town in southern Italy, built on a mountainside with some of the homes built into the cliff face as caves. For the scene the town had to be covered in snow with more falling. The special effects supervisor, Kit West, used foam for the snow in the distance, with paper dust as falling snow in the middle distance, sprayed with water so it would stick. For the close-up it would be salt or marble dust. It did look good but wouldn't be considered nowadays as there are specialist companies you can call upon who do the job in a much more environmentally friendly way. There were quite a lot of problems on this film, which had a limited release, but it was a job and we made the best of our time working on it.

Spies Like Us

Spies Like Us (1985) was directed by John Landis and starred Chevy Chase and Dan Aykroyd, with a cameo from Frank Oz. On this film I happily shared the production design credits with Peter Murton.

A particularly tricky job we had to sort out was a missile launcher that had to be mobile. I remembered seeing missile launchers with their carriers in a Red Square parade and wondered where we could get something like that. Driving along a motorway one day I spotted a large mobile crane being transported and I wondered if we could perhaps adapt something similar. I checked around and contacted a Bradford-based crane hire company who just happened to have exactly the model we wanted in for a service, which would take six months to complete. As its 16-axle carrier would be out of commission for all that time, we could hire it for the basis of our rocket launcher.

Special effects supervisor Brian Johnson and special effects engineer Mike Hope worked with me to figure out how we could make it happen. Thanks to the combined efforts of their crew, the art department and the production office, we got a very convincing missile launcher off to Norway for the shoot. However, the route it had to travel was along a tricky mountain road. The driver was convinced it would be OK but we nearly lost it on one sharp bend in thick snow and icy conditions. A young special effects man came to

Sketch showing the conversion of the crane transporter into a rocket launcher.

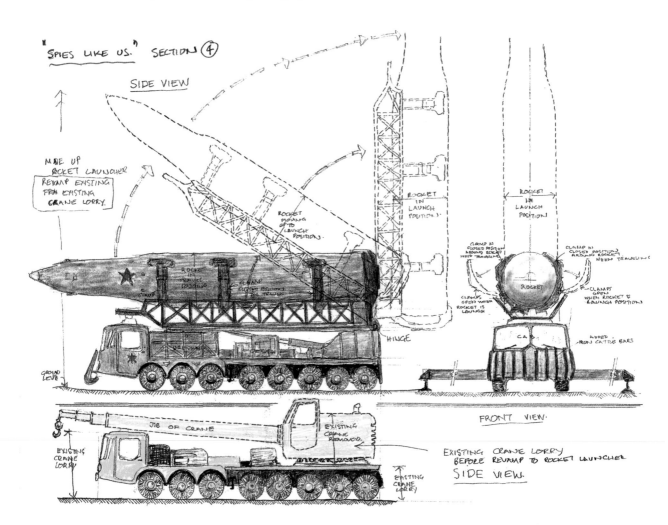

the rescue and was completely unfazed by the situation. He said all we had to do was use the carrier's hydraulic stabilisers, put plastic bags underneath and slide the whole thing around the bend. We had fingers and everything else crossed but it worked, clever lad!

The rocket launcher in the firing position and prepped for action.

Spies Like Us location recce in Austria.

Spies Like Us with the missile in the freezing Austrian Alps.

Labyrinth

I worked with Jim Henson and production designer Elliot Scott again on *Labyrinth* (1986). This was a film that tested everything we knew about design and construction, but thankfully we had an excellent art department and an amazing special effects team, plus the brilliant director of photography Alex Thomson and the equally brilliant storyboard artist Martin Asbury.

The sets were constructed at Elstree Studios in the UK and were quite a challenge! Building the labyrinth itself involved using a lot of perspective, which was put to very effective use when Sarah, played by Jennifer Connolly, first enters the set and tries to make her way to the castle where her baby brother is being held by the Goblin King, played by David Bowie. This was tricky enough but the biggest design and build problem we had was the staircase sequence with Sarah's baby brother making his way around what appears to be a very dangerous staircase. The Goblin King had to appear to step off and under the staircase, hanging upside down but looking as though he was firmly standing on a stair. For this the special effects team created a harness so that David Bowie could walk off the edge perfectly safely. Something like this would probably be done in post-production by the visual effects team nowadays and would be very expensive!

We called the stairs the Esher Set as they were going nowhere and had to look as though they were upside down as well as right side up. It was extremely complicated! Elliot had worked on it for quite some time but was unable to resolve the intricacies of the design, so he passed it on to me to see if I could do any better. I could only manage up to three sets of physical stairs as it was totally impossible to make it work with any more, so we eventually solved it by using huge, strategically placed mirrors to create the effect. It ended up as quite a big set, reaching 30ft high.

Sketch of the *Labyrinth* staircase (the Esher Set) showing the complicated design issues.

The Esher Set. A clever use of mirrors helped create the effect.

Aliens

On *Aliens* (1986) I was the supervising art director, working for production designer Peter Lamont and director James Cameron. For a particular sequence we needed an armoured personnel carrier with the steering set on the vertical, a bit like an old-fashioned truck with the steering column coming up through the floor of the vehicle. One day when I was at the airport I saw an aeroplane being manoeuvred by a tug and I thought that this could be just what we needed. The director wasn't sure about this until I borrowed one and he had a test drive. British Airways had a couple for sale so I bought one for £2,000.

Sketch showing the conversion of the airport tug into a personnel carrier for *Aliens*.

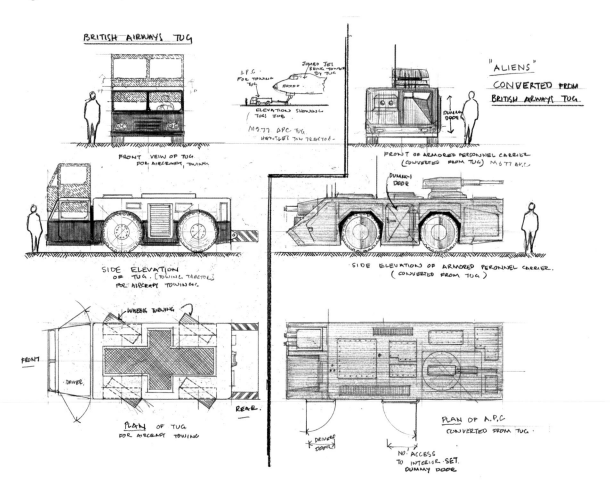

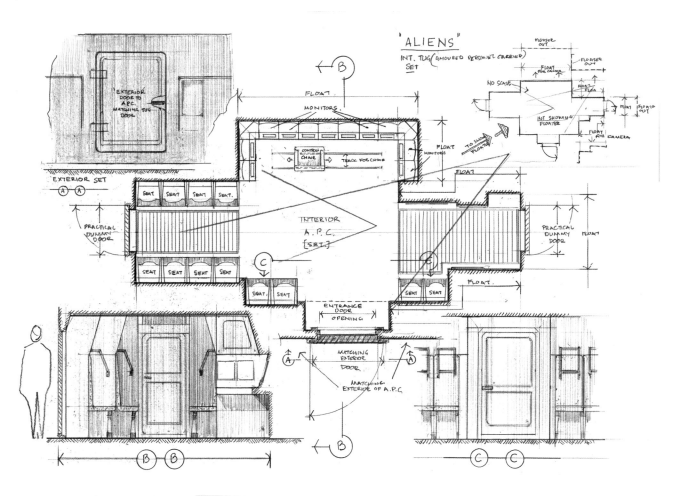

"ALIENS"
INT. TUG (ARMOURED PERSONNEL CARRIER) SET

Sketch of the interior of
the converted tug.

The finished vehicle.
*(Photo courtesy of
Rob Fodder)*

It was duly converted into the type of personnel carrier we needed but it wasn't possible to shoot inside the vehicle so we had to build the interior as a set. All the interiors for the sets of this vehicle, the drop ship and the atmosphere plant were made from parts of aircraft, old televisions, pallets and suchlike, picked up and reworked by set dressers Michael Lamont and Crispian Sallis with technical set dresser Mark Harris. They all worked very hard on this – very clever and inventive men! The drop ship cockpit's design was based on the interior of an RAF Hercules transport plane and the legs of the ship were the converted undercarriage of a jumbo jet – no wheels, just skids.

Sketch of Acton Power Station converted into an *Aliens* set.

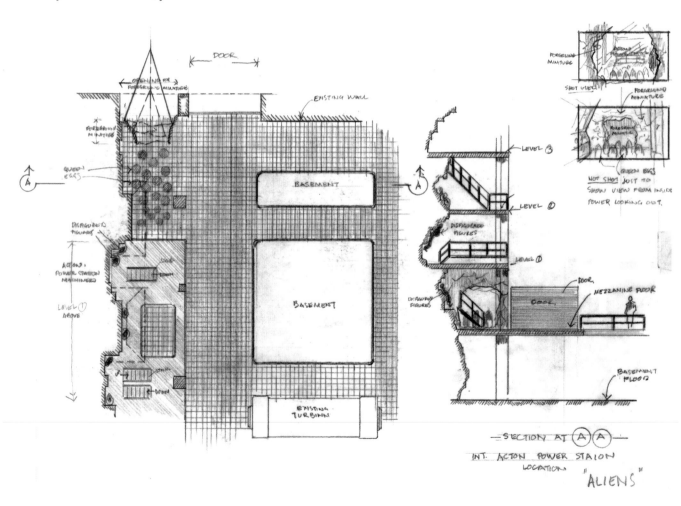

Inside the Acton Power Station set.

We had a lot of models on set and looking after all of them were two brothers from Los Angeles who the director had worked with before – Dennis and Robert Skotak.

For the atmosphere plant I thought that a disused power station might fit the bill, as on *Spies Like Us* we had used a decommissioned power station. I contacted the Electricity Board and they said that the one we had used had been demolished but that the Acton Power Station was due to be demolished soon so we could use it. This was much handier for access from Pinewood, just down the road! Everyone liked it as a location so Mark Harris and I made a model in order to plan the shots with the director and director of photography Adrian Biddle. In fact, it was such a successful location that we used it again with Tim Burton for *Batman*! Obviously, before we started work we had to get a specialist company in to remove all the asbestos, which took about three weeks to clear.

One of the art directors, Ken Court, was in charge of the foreground miniatures we were using at this location. A foreground miniature is a special effect similar to a matte shot but where a model, rather than a painting, is placed in the foreground, with the action taking place in the background. It is, in essence, a specific form of forced perspective. In one scene, the action goes through a cave entrance showing an egg nest, which is a miniature. As you travel further through the cave entrance, you enter the set built in the power station.

In one scene Bishop, played by Lance Henriksen, is attacked by the Queen inside the drop ship. The Queen's tail goes right through his body, splitting him in half. All this was done using special effects and puppets. We made a hole in the floor big enough for Bishop to fit into so that the camera could only see his torso, his legs being below floor level. It looked pretty gruesome on screen!

Sketch of the interior of the *Aliens* spaceship.

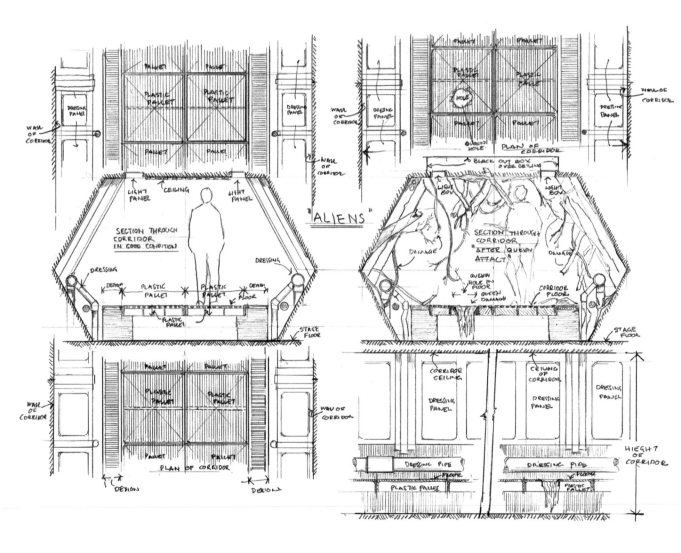

ART DIRECTOR AND SUPERVISING ART DIRECTOR

THE LIVING DAYLIGHTS

CONSUMING PASSIONS

BATMAN

The Living Daylights

The Living Daylights (1987) starred Timothy Dalton. I was supervising art director, working with director John Glen, director of photography Alec Mills and designer Peter Lamont. I was also working with a very good art director called Thomas Riccabona, who was such a great help to me on this job.

Peter sent me to Austria to find a particular theatre location, so I started off in Vienna looking at suitable venues. It was a successful trip and I found the ideal place, the Musikverein Concert Hall. We had to reproduce the theatre box back at Pinewood Studios so I took detailed measurements and pictures and sent them back to the art department. In the film it was the location where the sniper was supposed to take out the cellist played by Maryam D'Abo, who was defecting to the West, but the sniper was foiled by Bond, obviously!

In Vienna I had to organise the building of a stage dressed with flowers outside the Belvedere Palace, for a night shoot with dancers doing the Viennese waltz. The shoot took all night and I'd been there working the previous day as well, so I decided I needed a break. I found a little bar and enjoyed a well-deserved beer. As I left the bar who should be walking past but Barbara and Cubby Broccoli. They stopped and asked me if the beer was OK so, having been caught out, I sheepishly said it was fine.

'Good,' Cubby said. 'Let's go and have another!'

Later, on a different location up in the mountains, close to the border of Austria and Italy, when Cubby came to look at the location and the progress of the construction, he cooked lunch for the crew – squid and pasta. What a gent!

For the border control scene we needed to go and check out a working border. The interpreter and I travelled to the border between Austria and Bratislava for a recce. We arrived but had to wait our turn to be checked out by the officials so, while I was waiting, I started to sketch the buildings, make notes and do a quick plan of the crossing for reference. I sketched the massive barrier that was designed to take out large vehicles that might attempt to cross illegally, with the sand traps either side to show footprints of anyone trying to jump the fence.

While doing this I obviously didn't take proper notice of how thorough the border guards were as they took the car in front of us apart. They had dogs, guns and mirrors on sticks, all to stop any illegal entry. When it was our turn and they started checking the engine compartment and boot and removing the back seats, I had a moment of panic as my sketch pad was clearly visible on the dashboard. How on earth was I going to explain that I wasn't a spy, just making a film? Thankfully they didn't even notice it.

When we got to the passport control hut they said I couldn't go through as my passport photo wasn't a good likeness. In the passport I was clean shaven but, since it had been taken, I'd grown a rather lovely beard. I did suggest if they could loan me a razor I could shave it off but they insisted that I go to the British Embassy in Vienna and get a new picture. Off we went to sort it out and all they did at the Embassy was clip a new photo on top of the original, so we revisited border control later and got through with no trouble. What a drama!

It was a very strange experience going into Bratislava. It was Saturday, whenapparently every shop shuts down at lunchtime. All the lampposts were painted a different colour – red, blue, green and so on – and every shop window seemed to be dressed out the same with huge revolving flowers cut out of polystyrene, except for one department store that looked like a free-for-all car-boot sale.

We were a bit peckish so we found a small restaurant. I had been given about £200 of petty cash to buy reference books. I'd been told that I wouldn't be allowed to take any cash back over the border with me so, as there were no bookshops open, I thought we could have a damn good lunch. It was so cheap I decided to buy everyone's lunch in the restaurant – and I still had quite a lot of change left!

We built the border post on a bridge in Vienna with the Trans-Siberian gas pipeline running through the border. I must say that it looked very good when it was finished. As the story of the film went, the gas pipeline, which was about 3ft in diameter, was to be used to send our MI6 agent, fired in a capsule, across the border.

Setting up the gas pipeline, built on location on a glacier in Canada, for *The Living Daylights*.

Driving back to the airport for a quick visit to London, I noticed two huge round brick buildings and I asked my interpreter what they were. He said that there were just normal gasometers inside. The buildings must have been 200ft across and 200ft high, so I said that I would like to have a look at them when I got back. I got to see them on my return and I couldn't believe what I was seeing! Apparently, these brick structures were built by the British after the Second World War, with the gasometers inside. The lower brick walls were 12ft thick and going up the building was a gas pipeline, 3ft in diameter. I thought it would be a great location for a scene where a Harrier Jump Jet had to lift off, looking as though it was coming up through the roof. Access to the top was via a staircase, where there was still a very strong smell of gas and oil. I attempted to climb to the top but, having no head for heights, I had to stop halfway!

Of course, we couldn't do the proposed scene from the actual building so our photographer, Allan White, took shots from all angles. We then went to RAF Wittering in the UK, where the Harrier jet fighters were based and where they were allowing us use of one of the aeroplanes for a very short time. The photograph of the gasometers had been put onto Perspex and placed strategically on the runway so that, when the Harrier took off, it looked as though it was leaving the building through the roof as planned. It was all really well organised by the production office and the RAF, and it looked so good!

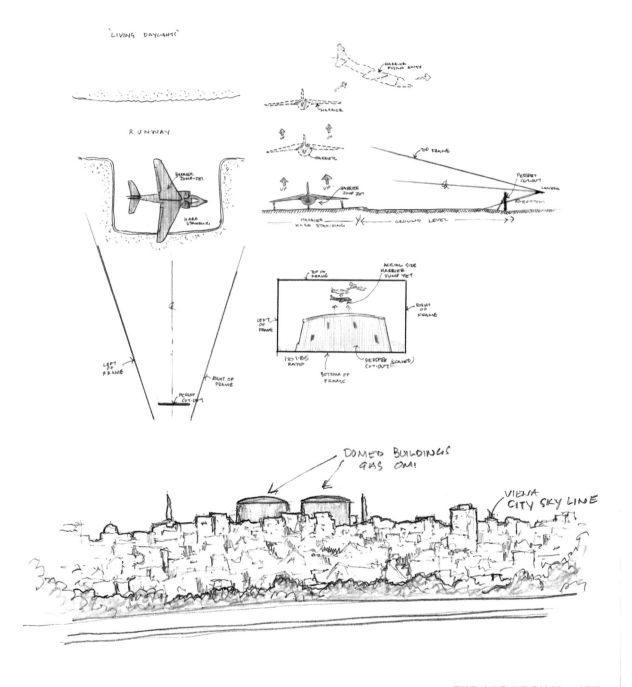

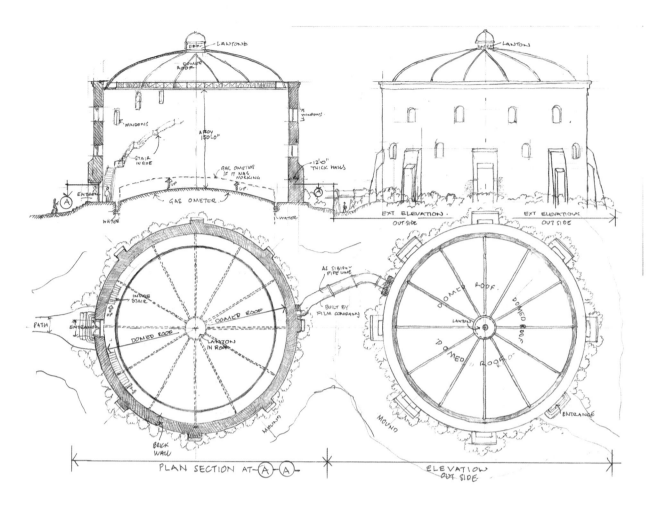

PLAN SECTION AT A–A

ELEVATION OUT SIDE

Sketches for the sequence with the Harrier jet rising out of the gasometer.

Me testing out the Harrier for the gasometer scene!

As a sneaky special treat before the shoot I asked if I could sit in the Harrier, which the RAF agreed to. It was a fantastic experience.

On location up in the Austrian mountains, there was a scene requiring the Aston Martin to drive across a frozen lake where the ice was around 12in thick. The car had to be fitted with skis, with one front nearside wheel without a tyre – just the rim, which would be used in the sequence to cut a hole in the ice. The car also had to enter a shed, drive around, exit, then mount a ramp and go through a guard house, smashing it to pieces.

As the director wanted to see the car flying through the air, a ramp was built on the iced-over lake. The ramp was 50ft long by 12ft high at the high end and was fixed to the ice on the lake. A gap of 45ft separated the ramp from the stunt boxes for the landing. The car had to travel at a speed of exactly 70mph to ensure height and accuracy when landing. However, the stuntman obviously got a bit too excited and drove the car at 90mph, only just making contact with the stunt boxes. He was a lucky man!

Sketches of the car jumping the lake in Austria.

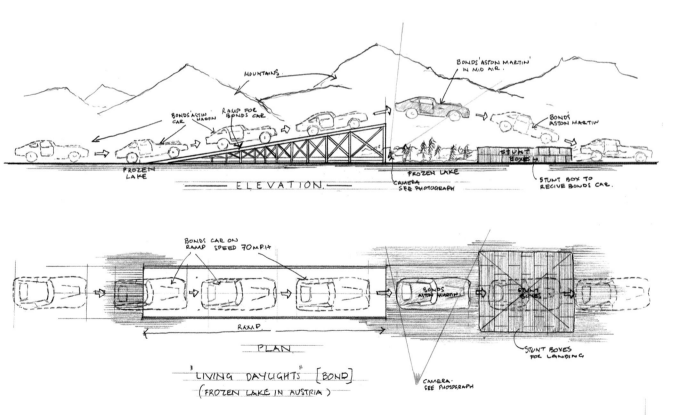

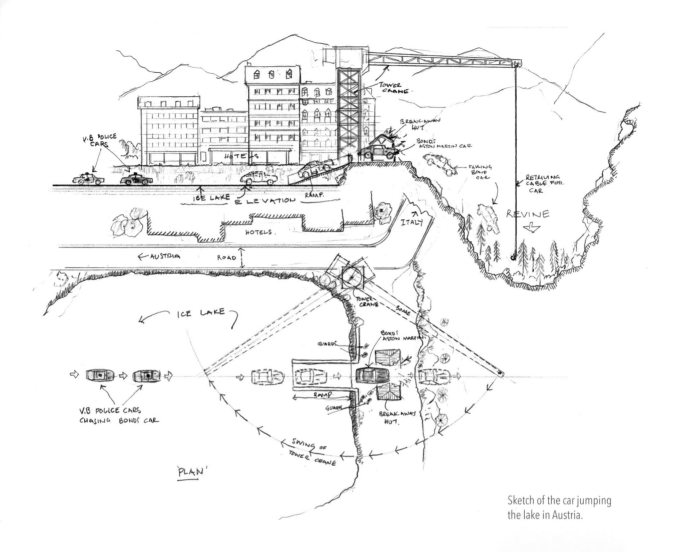

Sketch of the car jumping
the lake in Austria.

For the scene where Bond is being chased in the Aston Martin
through the snowy woods, we had to find a spot where we could
easily film the car hitting a tree and blowing up. John Richardson
from the special physical effects team, Barbara Broccoli and I went
on a Snowcat looking for a suitable location. A Snowcat has really
wide tracks so that it can manoeuvre easily over thick snow without
bogging down. We found what we thought would be a good place
and I decided to jump down and check it over properly. I wish I'd
listened to the driver, who did mention that it would be a bad idea,
but I thought to myself that it didn't look too bad. I went into the snow
almost up to my neck! When they stopped laughing and pulled me
out, the driver pointed out that, although the trees looked full size,
we were only seeing the tops. The rest was buried by the snow.

The location on the iced-over lake in Austria.

The action vehicle on the lake, complete with skids.

The ramp set up for take-off on the lake.

The car hoisted by a crane ready for another shot. Notice the skids on the far side.

Me with the camera operator planning the shot and making sure that the camera angle is OK.

As well as all the hard work involved, we had lots of fun doing this film. On one day off, a group of us - Derek Meddings, Terry Madden and some of the crew - went skiing on the nursery slopes, as recommended by John Richardson. There was a long rope with bars to haul us to the top with our skis on. Derek started to swing from side to side so we all did the same, laughing like a bunch of schoolboys. Once at the top we had to stand in a line but we were still laughing and when one of us fell over, we all fell down like dominoes. The poor ski instructor was trying to show us how to stop or slow down by 'ploughing'. Terry was first to go, only when he thought he was ploughing he just went faster and faster. At the bottom of the slope was a bank, which he hit at speed,

Sketch of the car exiting the Hercules mock-up for that iconic scene.

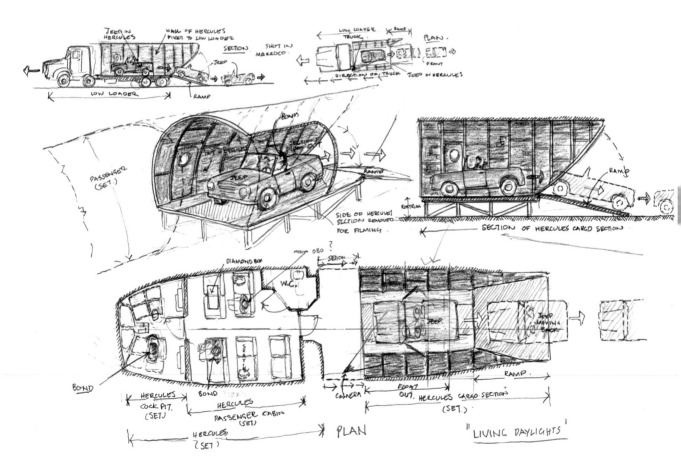

going up and over a small road and landing on a frozen lake. It was reminiscent of Eddie the Eagle! We all followed with varying degrees of competency, but we thoroughly enjoyed the day.

During filming, I had another ski adventure with John Richardson, his son and Barbara Broccoli. John and his son were competent skiers so had all the gear, while Barbara and I were just there as pedestrians. We went up in the chair lift. I must say that going over a very deep chasm wasn't a very pleasant experience but we made it to the top. John and his son were supposed to get off at the first stop, which was for the skiers, but they decided to wait until the next stop, which was for the pedestrians. It was a bad move as John ended up coming off into a pile of snow. All the gear but no idea comes to mind. I think he felt a proper fool!

Another fun day we had was playing snow golf. Yes, snow golf! I'd never heard of such a thing. You had to play with orange balls and the 'greens' were very fine snow flattened hard until it was almost like ice. The bunkers were rough snow piled up so you played just as you would on a normal course, except it was a bit colder and more slippery. The game was very competitive but great fun!

On the last day of shooting in Austria, I wasn't needed on set so I decided to spend the day resting in the hotel. It was a beautiful day up in the mountains and I was sitting on the veranda in the sun when I spotted Cubby coming up the path. He saw me and asked if I wanted a coffee. 'That would be nice,' I said, so he disappeared, only to reappear five minutes later with the coffees on a silver tray. He was such a lovely gentleman. Sadly we don't have a lot of producers as nice as that.

There was another scene in the movie, filmed in Morocco, where Timothy Dalton and Maryam D'Abo exited a Hercules military transport plane from the open loading ramp while the plane was in the air.

I didn't have anything to do with this set; it was built back at Pinewood Studios, the work of Peter Lamont, Jim Morahan and their team. Jim drew it up with every detail, including the cockpit. The amount of research he did was amazing. There was a lot of work involved in that scene for the crew and I think that it was one of the more memorable scenes in the film.

Consuming Passions

This was a low-budget film, released in 1988, where I worked as art director for designer Peter Lamont. The star was Tyler Butterworth (son of actor Peter Butterworth), along with Jonathan Pryce, Freddie Jones, Vanessa Redgrave, Thora Hird, Timothy West, Andrew Sachs and Linda Lusardi – quite a line-up!

The hero starts a new job at a chocolate factory and accidentally knocks several workers into a mixing vat, the contents of which is sent to market. The consumers like the chocolate with the 'special ingredient' and our hero is tasked with finding more.

It was filmed at Pinewood and we found a company near Heathrow Airport who were selling second-hand food mixers, vats and conveyor belts, which we used to dress the factory set. They weren't in working order but the special effects crew soon had them all going – teamwork again!

Batman

Tim Burton's *Batman* was a big film for me as an art director, working for production designer Anton Furst and alongside fellow art directors Nigel Phelps and Les Tomkins. We filmed at Pinewood Studios as well as various locations in the UK, with Hatfield House in Hertfordshire doubling up as Wayne Manor and both the Acton and Little Barfield power stations used as the Axis Chemical Works. It turned into an iconic film, winning Oscars for Anton Furst and set decorator Peter Young, with several more wins and nominations at other major awards ceremonies.

Before the film was greenlit I worked on the above- and below-the-line budgets with co-producer Chris Kenny, as Anton Furst was busy working on another film with Tim Burton. It took us around four months to complete. For the uninitiated, above-the-line generally includes producers, directors, performers and cinematographers. Below-the-line encompasses the rest of the crew – in fact the full working crew, including the art department.

Sketch of how we converted the Impala to the Batmobile.

Once the green light had been given, Anton Furst took me and Les Tomkins to lunch and asked us which part of the film we wanted to work on. I said that I would like to work on the construction of the Batmobile, probably the best prop to be involved with at that time. 'OK,' he said. 'You got it!' What great fun! It was also decided that Les should look after the sets and I should look after locations, with both of us working on the back-lot set of Gotham City. Les looked after the day shoots and I was tasked with looking after the night shoots, six weeks in all.

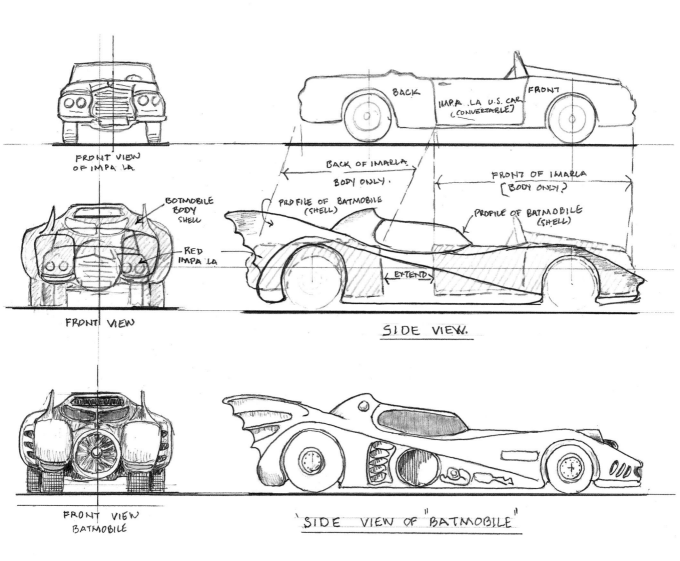

FRONT VIEW OF IMPALA

FRONT VIEW

BATMOBILE BODY SHELL

RED IMPALA

BACK

IMPALA U.S. CAR (CONVERTABLE)

FRONT

BACK OF IMARLA BODY ONLY.

FRONT OF IMARLA (BODY ONLY)

PROFILE OF BATMOBILE (SHELL)

PROFILE OF BATMOBILE (SHELL)

EXTEND

SIDE VIEW.

FRONT VIEW BATMOBILE

'SIDE VIEW OF "BATMOBILE"

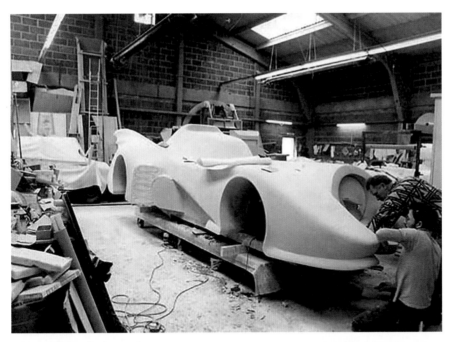

The Batmobile
under construction.

Some of the team who
worked with me (in the
striped shirt) on the
Batmobile. Left to right:
John Lovell, Andy Holder,
Keith Short, and front:
Julian Callow.

We had quite a few obstacles to overcome, not least of which was the Batmobile! We contacted a major motor manufacturer in Detroit but were told that it would take them around three years to custom-build a vehicle, so we had to think again. We bought a couple of Impala drophead cars (one pink and one yellow) and used the chassis as a base. While we were constructing the vehicle and working on the distinctive body shape in polystyrene, Tim Burton came in and commented, 'Great, but how do they get in the car? There aren't any doors!' Sadly, I hadn't thought of that. However, I'd recently been in a Harrier with its sliding hood, so it gave me an idea. Special effects supervisor John Evans custom-built a tricky hydraulic mechanism to make the hood work properly. I found larger-than-life petrol caps on a London Routemaster bus and based the rear lights on those of a Ferrari, while the dashboard was based on the shape of the Batwing. At the time I had a BMW where a lot of the controls faced the driver, so I did the same for the Batmobile. We completed the whole build in four months!

Batman, played by Michael Keaton, had to sit in the car, so we had Recaro seats fitted. Unfortunately, when Michael was fully dressed in the hood, complete with ears, the ears hit the roof and were bent forward just a little, so Tim asked if I could lower the seat. However, we were almost at the limit of how low the seat could go as there was very little clearance on the car. Eventually Bob Ringwood, the costume designer, solved the problem by making a Batmobile hood for the costume with slightly shorter ears. There are so many small problems on film sets that the viewer never notices, but the crew have to overcome. This demonstrates exactly how a good film crew should work together, each department making sure that the finished product is the best it can be.

I had nothing to do with the Bat Cave, as Les Tomkins was looking after that. It was like the inside of a coal mine: very dark with lots of rock strata and rocky shelves. We had to use a crane to move the Batmobile onto one of these shelves. When Les and Peter Young were showing me around the set one day, I noticed a white spot on one of the shelves, but Peter said he couldn't see any white spot. Just then Tim Burton arrived to check out the set and he also noticed the white spot and asked Peter what it was. 'Oh,' said Peter. 'I see it now.' He shouted at a propman up on high, 'OK, Sid, you can lift the cat up now!' It was a stuffed cat on wires which Peter had organised to attract the director's attention and perhaps take his mind off noticing anything wrong with the Bat Cave – but of course the set was OK. Clever Peter!

A sketch of the *Batman* set for an action sequence in Acton Power Station.

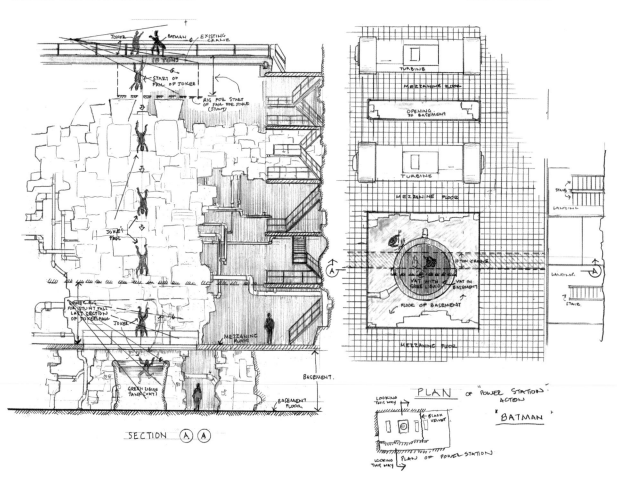

We built the Gotham City street on the Pinewood back lot. It was a quarter of a mile long, with alleyways, a town square, a town hall, the exterior of a museum and the base of a cathedral, all looked after by Les Tomkins with construction manager Terry Apsey.

I was charged with looking after the night shoots, so I would meet Les early in the mornings to let him know of any extra requirements. For example, sometimes we needed more of the Joker's fleet of cars, which were all painted exactly the same in his colours.

The set had lots of neon signs that we had to organise but Tim Burton thought that they were too bright and colourful so asked if I could dim them down a bit. Believe it or not, the answer was hairspray – nowadays we'd just put less gas in the tubes!

The Gotham City street under construction.

Aerial shot of the Gotham City street built on the Pinewood back lot.

Prepping a helicopter for an action shot.

Les Tomkins and me
standing in the street
ready for a night shoot.

PRODUCTION DESIGNER

THE RAINBOW THIEF
INSPECTOR MORSE
SOLDIER SOLDIER
THE DOOMSDAY GUN
CLOSING NUMBERS
MONSIGNOR RENARD
COMMAND APPROVED

The Rainbow Thief

The Rainbow Thief (1990) was shot at Shepperton and on location in Poland. It starred Peter O'Toole and Omar Sharif, who had worked together on *Lawrence of Arabia*, as well as Christopher Lee. The story was about a petty crook in search of the fabled pot of gold at the end of the rainbow, hoping to cash in by befriending the heir to a huge fortune.

Sketch of the breakaway tank sequence for *The Rainbow Thief*.

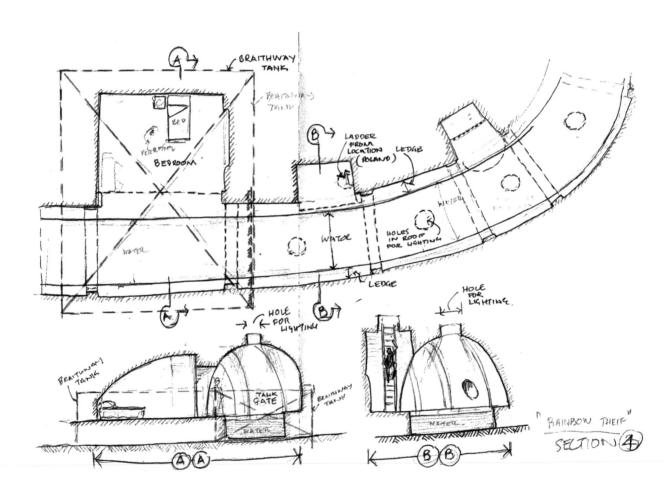

Again I was working with set dresser Peter Young. The main set was a sewer in France which had to be flooded. The whole set was built in a tank on one of the stages at Shepperton, where Peter O'Toole's character had his home. The set had to flood to about 5ft deep. We couldn't flood the whole set so we built his home with dam doors so that we could control the water levels.

The director was Alejandro Jodorowsky, who had a really interesting background. We had a little difficulty with language but it all worked out in the end.

Inspector Morse

This popular television series in the 1990s starred John Thaw as Chief Inspector Morse and Kevin Whately as Detective Sergeant Lewis. I was production designer for seven series and it was quite a challenging job. Particularly time consuming was looking after Morse's car, a Jaguar Mark 2, which featured heavily in the series. It wasn't initially in very good order, so in one scene when John Thaw was in the vehicle and went to wind down the window, the handle came off in his hand and the window fell right down.

That was only the start of so many things going wrong! In one episode, called 'Masonic Mysteries', the car had to have the masonic symbol scratched onto the bodywork, without actually damaging the vehicle itself. Luckily I had a young assistant called Stephen Scott who set to work making the symbol by cutting out sticky Fablon strips that could be easily removed without any damage.

As the shooting continued, the leather seating started to look a little tired, so the producer David Lascelles asked if we could have it renovated after shooting had finished. I found a Jaguar restoration specialist who was advertising his services in a motoring magazine, so I took the car to him and he started working on it. About two months later David asked how the work was going on the car but, to be quite honest, I'd almost forgotten about it because I was working on another film at the time. When I went to see the restorer to check on progress, the car was in pieces scattered around his workshop – wings, bonnet, doors and so on.

Inspector Morse cast and crew.

A miniature used in *Inspector Morse*.

However, he assured me that the car would be ready for delivery in two weeks and, true to his word, it came back looking like new with all the interior completely refurbished.

During the series we had the help of a very good police advisor, which was welcome as the art department had to fabricate all the warrant cards and official documents. As it happened the advisor had just retired and lived very close to me, which was very handy.

In one sequence the interior of Morse's apartment had to catch fire. I suggested that we should build a set at Pinewood, which we successfully set on fire, and it saved a lot of time.

Soldier Soldier

I was production designer on the television series *Soldier Soldier*, which first aired in 1991. On the very first episode there was a scene where two soldiers had a fight in a rubbish dump. There was meant to be a pile of 'live' rubbish, which meant household waste, but I didn't much like the idea of this! The pile had to be very high, about 20ft, so I designed a pyramid structure that was dressed with black plastic bags not filled with household waste. Lucy Gannon was the writer and originator of the series. She had previously been a nurse and it was her first job, so she was a bit bothered about us having to do this, saying that she wouldn't have written that scene if she had known it would cause any difficulty. I tried to put her mind at rest and said that it was my job to solve the problems so she should write whatever was in her mind to make the story work.

On location in Germany there was a sequence in which there was an exercise using tanks, at least six Warriors and four Centurions, with the troops debussing (leaving the tanks). Robson Green, Jerome Flynn and Gary Love were travelling in a Warrior when it had to go out of control and turn upside down. A real tank would be too heavy (about 30–40 tons) but we did acquire a stripped-out tank, which made it a lot lighter, probably about 15 tons.

The camera crew on a
Warrior tank.

Camera crew and cast in
Germany ready for action.

The camera crew with
director of photography
Alec Mills.

Me checking out the tank!

Checked the outside, now
for the interior!

The tank had to be pushed down an embankment into the river and turned upside down. Having been stripped out and therefore not having any means of propulsion, it had to be pushed by another tank, all organised by technical special effects supervisor Ian Wingrove. There was a problem, however, as we had to do all of this on army property because the roadways had to be substantial enough to carry the weight of the tanks. There wasn't a river in sight, just a small field at the bottom of the bank. We made our own 'river' by digging a hole in the field and putting a very large black pond liner at the bottom, filling it with water and dressing the edges with reeds and other vegetation. It was a night shot and worked out extremely well.

We had to build the interior of the upside-down Warrior as a breakaway set hanging over a water tank. 'Breakaway' means destroyable scenery or props; in this case it means that the wall of the military tank could be removed to allow camera access. The set was rigged so that the tank could be lowered into the water for the interior shots. It worked very well and it did look dramatic.

The director who had planned this sequence left suddenly at the eleventh hour. I was fully aware of what was planned so when the new director arrived from London, obviously without much idea of what was going on, he asked me to help. I went through the plan with the major who was helping us and it all turned out OK. We had good fun that day! This is a prime example of not only understanding your job but also needing to know how it interacts with others.

Another set was a mock-up of a guard house which we built within the barracks. The structure was made in the UK, then shipped out and erected on site. It looked so good when it was finished that the soldiers thought we'd built them a new guard house.

On location in Hong Kong, I needed a set decorator to join me. My first choice was Peter Young but he couldn't fly out for a few months so he recommended Malcolm Stone. I'd never worked with Malcolm before so I was a bit unsure but Peter had already put him on the plane, so I guessed he must be OK!

When Malcolm landed after the long flight, he was obviously hot and tired, but he had a meeting with us straight away. We all had our fingers crossed that it was going to work out. I needn't have worried as the first set he dressed, a very feminine bedroom, was really good. Everyone was impressed and breathed a sigh of relief. Malcolm and I have been friends ever since and we've worked together on many other films.

While I was in Hong Kong I had the privilege of being taken for a trip on a Royal Navy landing craft to check it out for an episode. It was much bigger than I'd imagined and was capable of carrying 400 troops or two Warrior tanks. Each craft had its identification number painted on the hull. Down the centre of the craft was a painted yellow line that the skipper would use as a steering guide as his cockpit was at the rear. He asked if I would like to have a go at steering. 'Oh, yes please,' I said. He told me to keep the guideline on any landmark and to keep the craft straight. Much easier said than done! I presumed it was like steering any other boat, starboard to the right and port to the left. My problem was the yellow line wouldn't stay in line with the landmark. When it went off course, I would spin the wheel to left or right to get back on course, but it was very slow in responding so when my yellow line was in line with the target, it would keep on turning! The skipper wryly asked if I liked zigzagging. He told me to take a look behind me, where the wake was making a very distinct and, I think, quite pretty, pattern. It was a brilliant experience, but I doubt if I'll ever be asked to join the fleet!

On location in Hong Kong with set dresser Malcolm Stone.

On location in Hong Kong, left to right: production manager Ann Tricklebank, me, director Nick Hamm and producer Chris Kelly.

Me with Ann Tricklebank and Sharon Houleghan, off on a recce!

The production manager, Ann Tricklebank, had organised a landing craft for the day of the shoot so she and I went down to the beach at 5 a.m. to wait for it to arrive. It didn't show up until 7 a.m. and, to my horror, it was another boat with a different identity number. We had already used the original craft for a previous sequence, so the identity number had to match for continuity. Malcolm came to the rescue and we changed the numbers on the boat, which were around 6ft tall, with Fablon strips. Thank goodness for Fablon!

While we were in Hong Kong we were searching for alleyways that hadn't been used in another series that had been shot there, *Yellowthread Street*. Apparently the production team on that series had been told by a local and much-feared gang to pay $60,000, otherwise they would make it impossible for them to shoot the scenes – so we decided to look elsewhere and eventually found much safer places!

One of the things I liked to do after shooting was finished on every location was buy a drink for all the locals who had helped as a little extra 'thank you'. On the last day, I was a little late out of a meeting and was driving in a truck with Malcolm Stone, who wanted to drop by a plant nursery on the way as he needed some set dressing for that day in the village. It was closed and there was no one about so we could do no more than nip in and load what he wanted onto the truck, then we closed the gates again and went on our way.

When we got to the evening, instead of the six or so people we expected, there must have been at least thirty and they'd arranged a meal as well. The meal wasn't exactly what I would order in a Chinese restaurant and we were expected to eat it all, eyes and shells and other bits and pieces. The worst of all was the chicken's feet, which had been boiled and were a bit slimy. I tried so hard to avoid eating any but they saved the last one for me and watched me eat it!

However, they were lovely people and we had a very nice time with them. Being nice and honest people, we dropped all the greenery off at the nursery on the way back and secured the gate properly, a kind of 'loan' that I hope the production office paid for.

For another scene, we were in the officers' mess in Windsor for a formal dinner sequence, with the table laid out with all the military silver. When it came to the shoot the cameraman suggested it would be nice to have some ambient light coming in through the window. The problem was the scene was supposed to take place at night and we had blacked out all the windows. We had to build a large blackout tent over the window so he could set up his ambient light effect.

Sketch of the mess hall.

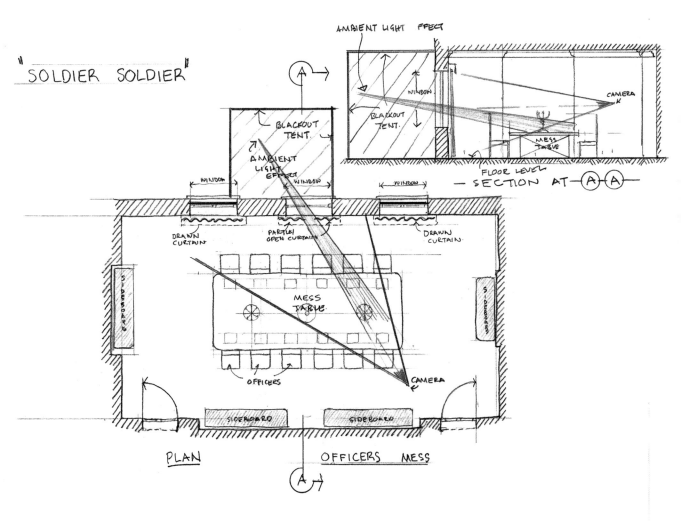

"SOLDIER SOLDIER"

AMBIENT LIGHT EFFECT

CAMERA

WINDOW

BLACKOUT TENT.

MESS TABLE

FLOOR LEVEL
— SECTION AT (A)(A)

BLACKOUT TENT.

AMBIENT LIGHT EFFECT

WINDOW   WINDOW   WINDOW

DRAWN CURTAIN   PARTLY OPEN CURTAIN   DRAWN CURTAIN

SIDEBOARD   MESS TABLE   SIDEBOARD

OFFICERS   CAMERA

SIDEBOARD   SIDEBOARD

PLAN   OFFICERS MESS
(A)

The cast and crew of *Soldier Soldier*.

For an episode shot in Cyprus we were on an RAF base in Akrotiri where our characters had to disembark from a Hercules aircraft. There was one major problem: the base didn't have a Hercules on site. However, our production office got to work and found out that the base was expecting a Hercules en route from Iraq to land for fuelling on a specific day, although it was only going to be on the ground for thirty minutes. The RAF agreed to let us have access while it was there, but for only fifteen minutes. We rehearsed the scene thoroughly, minus aircraft but with camera and lighting. The film accountant came out to see the shoot and had obviously never seen a camera set-up before, so asked what the 'railway' was for. Once I explained all about the camera tracking rail, along with the Elemack dolly, he was delighted. Apparently he'd always wondered what these strange gadgets were that he was signing off on the budget!

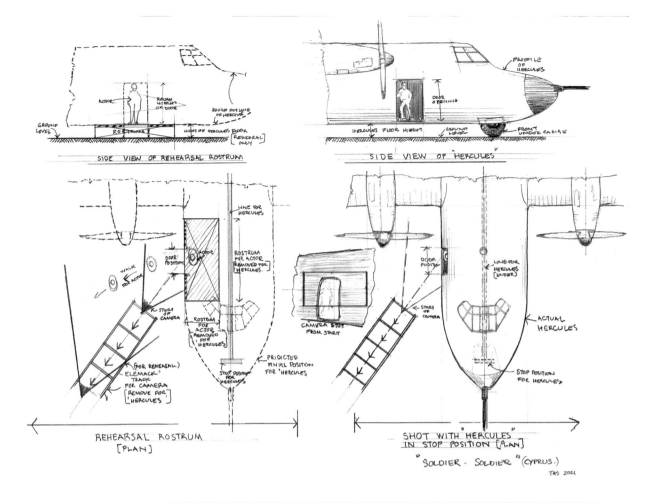

SIDE VIEW OF REHEARSAL ROSTRUM

SIDE VIEW OF "HERCULES"

REHEARSAL ROSTRUM
[PLAN]

SHOT WITH "HERCULES"
IN STOP POSITION [PLAN]

"SOLDIER - SOLDIER" (CYPRUS.)

TRS 2021

Sketch of the preparation for shooting the sequence with the Hercules transport plane.

Rehearsing inside the Chinook helicopter.

For another episode we were shooting in Aldershot, the home of the British Army. The scene required a location with a swimming pool, which we found, but it hadn't been used for a considerable time. There was standing water in the pool, which made it not suitable for swimming; however, the architecture was magnificent! The foyer of the building was hexagonal with a balcony running around it, which was accessed by a cast-iron spiral staircase. The army had painted over the original tiled walls that, when uncovered, were beautiful and brightly coloured. It took a lot of paint stripper and three long weeks but we got them looking beautiful. We painted the cast-iron staircase orange to complement the peacock-blue and green tiles. Once finished it looked amazing but when I went back a couple of months later they'd painted over the tiles again. What a travesty!

At an army barracks near Lyndhurst, we had a scene where a soldier, played by James Nesbitt, was sitting in a car outside a house in the married quarters when the car blew up. The house we'd selected had a very high hedge. Of course, we couldn't blow a car up outside an actual house and it was not a very good idea to set up an explosion so close to the barracks – who knows what mayhem we might have caused – so we went to a disused car park and put up a false hedge to match the one in front of the house. We put a dummy in the car so that the special effects team could do their work. It was very loud; my ears were ringing for hours afterwards.

Back at the barracks we had extras as soldiers with SA80 rifles – not real ones but plastic replicas from Japan, much lighter and easier for the extras to manage. When they'd finished with them the armourer and prop men had to check them all in. We couldn't have any going astray for safety reasons, as even though they were replicas, they looked far too real for comfort.

For one sequence we had to blow up a café, which sounds easy but isn't. The café had to be made so that it imploded, as if it had exploded it would have covered everyone nearby with splinters. It was all done strictly to the special effects team's directions. All the dressings inside the café – tables, table dressings and chairs – had to be prepared properly. It was a nightmare for us and it just shows how much effort goes into a shot that is over in seconds. Such a lot of work was put into that set for a few moments on screen.

The Doomsday Gun

The Doomsday Gun (1994) was about the brilliant Canadian munitions engineer Dr Gerald Bull, who in 1988 agreed to build Saddam Hussein a supergun that was capable of firing over 100 miles. When a plan by the CIA to use Bull to export restricted material was exposed, the CIA denied all knowledge and he went to jail. He was later released to help Saddam Hussein build the supergun. Israel, learning of the supergun, feared it would be used against them.

The director was Robert Young. I'm not convinced that I was his first choice on this film – I think he would have preferred Martin Childs, who wasn't available at that time – which, of course, made my job a little more difficult.

Searching for a suitable location for the build of the gun involved a lot of travelling through the mountains in Tunisia, finally ending up in Almería in Spain. I was travelling with line producer Malcolm Christopher. We were staying in a 5-star hotel in Tunisia, which was very nice, but we had to drive around 300–400 miles across the desert, going through a few villages en route. We had been advised not to stop for security reasons but we had to fill up with petrol at one village. I was so hungry but I'd been advised not to eat local food as our European digestive systems found it hard to handle.

Travelling on the recce for a suitable location for the *Doomsday Gun* build.

Rush hour at the local train station.

I did manage to buy some bread and I began to understand why Malcolm had told me to eat as much breakfast as I could manage in the hotel before we set off!

During the journey I spotted a lot of poles that appeared to have rags flying from them. When I asked the interpreter he said that they were prayer flags. At another point, we had to stop at a small town that had a train station. When a train pulled in, there was utter pandemonium, with everyone rushing and pushing to get on. It was fascinating to watch.

We were booked into another lovely hotel at an oasis, which is a welcome sight in the middle of a desert - green bushes, palm trees and lots of water. It was extremely hot and we were very thankful for the hotel's air conditioning and swimming pool after a long drive.

Drawing of the supergun build.

We eventually arrived at the location where we were intending to build the supergun but, after checking it thoroughly, I thought it wouldn't be suitable as the sand was far too soft to hold the weight of the gun. It was a big decision for an art director and designer to make. We eventually shot the scene in Andalucía in Spain, although the area was quite overgrown so we needed it cleared. To my amazement the local authorities agreed to bulldoze the area for us!

The director and I went to Bristol to visit the ballistics engineer, who had worked on the actual gun. This gave me a great opportunity to find out exactly what the gun looked like. He asked if I would like to see some original drawings and said that he had about 14,000 in

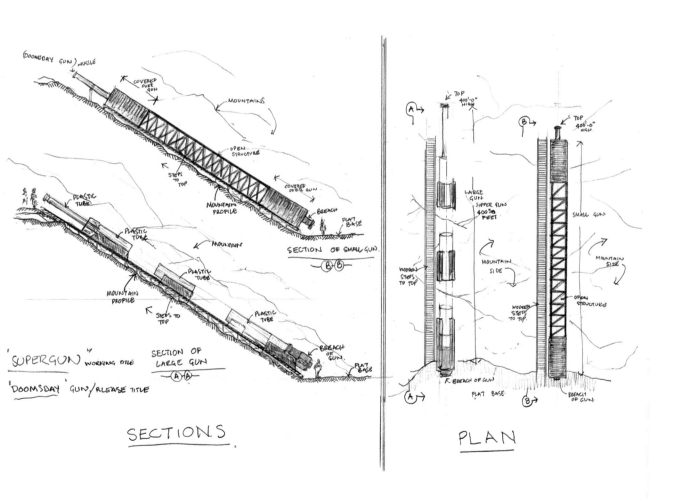

Left and opposite: The gun under construction on location in Spain.

all. He disappeared into another room and came back with drawings of the breech and the workings as well as colour photographs of the finished gun. What a find! He actually said that I could take them with me provided his agent gave the OK, but it would cost £500, so I quickly rang the production office to release the cash!

I gave the drawings to art director Fred Hole, who did many more drawings for us. We started construction of the gun in a farmyard close to Pinewood Studios. The gun was 400ft long and was looked after by the construction manager, Alan Booth. He finished the whole thing off on location in Spain and I'm told the local labour force were prisoners from a nearby jail.

One tricky sequence involved a 15ft poster of Saddam Hussein, fitted on a metal frame and placed on the roadside. The locals objected very strongly so we had to lower it face-down and only raise it when the time came for the shoot.

Closing Numbers

This was a low-budget film starring Tim Woodward and Jane Asher. I was the designer, working alongside director Stephen Whittaker and cinematographer Nic Knowland. The script required a small flat eleven floors up in a tower block overlooking London. The idea was that you could see St Paul's and the Houses of Parliament out of the window, as the actor was supposed to be doing the washing up in the kitchen, saying something like, 'Look at this amazing view over London. If you had a flat in the building next to this, seeing the same view, it would cost you £3 million and I only pay affordable rent!'

I went on the recce with the director and we found a flat with the view as required. He asked if it worked for me but I had to say that it didn't. The kitchen was very small and there would be no room to shoot as the camera crew wouldn't have enough space to get kit and crew in with room to manoeuvre. I said that we'd be better off building a set back at the studio but the lady who was guiding us around said she had two flats that had been knocked together on the ground floor, which meant that we would have enough room but no view.

Checking out the camera angles for *Closing Numbers*.

I came up with the idea that we could use a translight backing on the outside of the window. I'd been told about this method by an American art director when I was working on *Half a Sixpence*. It's a large, illuminated photographic backing, typically used as a backdrop, which is lit from behind. We could use it on the ground-floor flat and no one would know it wasn't an actual view of London when it was on screen. We discussed it with the cinematographer and decided to give it a go, and it worked!

Monsignor Renard

Monsignor Renard (2000) was a television drama series set during the Second World War, starring John Thaw and produced by Chris Kelly. There was such a lot of research involved in this and I did recces all over France with a French location manager. We were looking for a suitable village with a square that looked right for the period, which we eventually found in Saint-Valery-sur-Somme. Although the village did have a square, there was a huge rose garden in the centre, which didn't fit our purposes. Having cleared it with the town officials, we called in a local garden centre to remove and store the roses so that they could be replaced at the end of filming. We covered the area with rubber cobblestones, which I managed to find at Pinewood, to make the square look right for the period. Rubber cobblestones are used so that they can be easily removed afterwards; also, if you're using horses, the sound of the hooves doesn't interfere with the sound on set, and they don't slip and slide about as they would if real cobblestones were used.

One problem was that, although the buildings around the square were perfect, they were only on three sides, so we had to build matching frontages on the fourth side. This posed a little problem as there were quite strong winds around at the time and anchoring down the frontages proved to be a bit of a headache.

The village worked very well for us as there was no evidence of modern fixings. We shipped in most of the period vehicles, both French and German, from the UK. For a later episode there was a snow scene, which we shot in July, so we had a UK company come out and dress the set.

Sketch of the village location for *Monsignor Renard*.

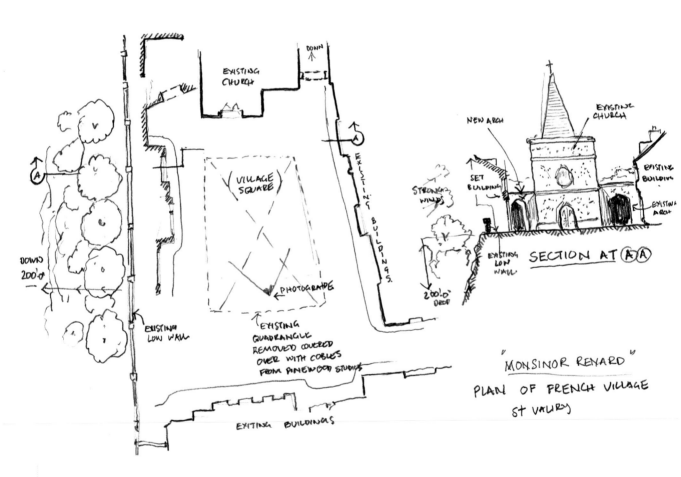

The village square.

For one episode we needed a steam train but the only one available to us was in Paris at the time. I went to check it out but the engine was in pieces. However, they assured me that it could be up and running in six weeks and, true to their word, it was! It took several days to get to our location as it was a single line so it had to pop into sidings along the way to let other trains pass, but the filming at an old railway station worked out really well. The whole of the art department crew worked so well on this: construction manager Alan Booth with set dresser Malcolm Stone and art directors James Lewis and Desmond Crow. They were all great.

We had to stage a scene where a lot of refugees in old cars and horse-drawn carts, carrying furniture and other household goods, were trying to flee along a road and were strafed by a Messerschmitt Me 109 with bullet hits and explosions. You'll have seen a lot of original footage of this happening during the Second World War. The location was a road near Le Touquet, which was near to the airport. The explosions were staged by the special physical effects unit led by Ian Wingrove. It was quite a tricky operation as we only had one shot at it so it had to be rehearsed a lot to make sure it all worked out perfectly. The plane was flown in from the UK. It was the first assistant's job to coordinate all this on his radio to the pilot – up a bit, down a bit, left and right – so that the plane was in exactly the right place for the camera to capture the action.

The refugees on the road being strafed by a Messerschmitt Me 109.

Command Approved

I worked as production designer on *Command Approved* (2000), directed by Graham Moore. We filmed in the Bahamas on an island called Eleuthera, which means 'The Island of Freedom'. This film was commissioned by the Royal Navy and was shown for around eighteen years at Portsmouth Naval Base's historic dockyard, as it demonstrates what the Royal Navy has to deal with in a conflict situation and shows action with helicopter, ship and weapons simulators.

The basic plot has a Type 23 frigate (HMS *Monmouth* and HMS *Montrose* were used in the action) receiving a distress call from a merchant vessel that has a cargo of gold bullion and is under attack from pirates. The crew of the frigate find themselves drawn into the struggle with the lives of hostages at stake.

I went first to recce on my own, armed with a camcorder, and once I'd shown Graham the footage he gave the OK. The second time he came out with me and a BBC production manager to choose the specific locations. The production manager organised a fixed-wing aircraft for us to fly over a chosen site. I strongly suggested a helicopter as it would be much easier to manoeuvre and hover over places that we wanted to check thoroughly, but I was told it was too expensive. I particularly wanted to show Graham a villa. At first the villa was on the port side but by the time Graham had focused out of the window, we had passed it, so it took several uncomfortable passes until he had fully assessed the site.

Back in the UK I started to put my team together, headed by art director Malcolm Stone.

I went to Portsmouth to check out a destroyer that was going to be used in the Bahamas. It had to be able to do a 45° turn. I was on the bridge with the commander and he asked if I got seasick, as during the turn the ship would tilt quite severely. Luckily I was OK and didn't show myself up!

During one scene, special effects coordinator Peter Hutchinson was on a frigate to look after the firing of a Harpoon missile to deal with an incoming target. Peter had put together a dummy missile, which looked very convincing. When fired it was supposed to travel about 300yd and then drop into the sea, but somehow it turned around and headed back to the ship. This caused the commander to turn slightly white - but it was only a dummy and dropped harmlessly into the sea long before it reached the ship.

There's a scene in the film where a convoy on land is travelling through woodland. The palm trees were 60ft high but, in spite of their height, when a special effects explosion went off, some of the fronds at the top caught alight. It was quite a sight, but not exactly what we intended! We had organised the local fire brigade to be on standby but when the time came for them to leap into action they were already packing up their hoses ready to go home. The fire chief said that they were going to a fish barbecue and weren't about to miss it, so it was all hands to the pumps as we joined Peter and his crew to douse the flames.

However, when we were in the Bahamas, I became very ill with kidney stones and had to return to the UK for an operation before shooting finished, so Malcolm took over the film. We had already gone through the whole project in great detail so everyone was fully informed. Sadly, I didn't recover in time and never returned to the island.

FILMS THAT DIDN'T
MAKE IT TO THE SCREEN

LONE WOLF AND CUB
THE MERCENARIES
JACK THE RIPPER

There are many films and television programmes, in various stages of production, that don't make it onto the screen. We've all been involved in a good few of these throughout our careers; here are three of mine that I nearly worked on in the 1990s.

Lone Wolf and Cub

This film was set in the USA so I flew to Los Angeles and then on to Pasadena, where I stayed in a rented house with the director and the storyboard artist Mike Ploog. The house was a little creepy, much like the one in *The Silence of the Lambs*, and I must say that I was a little nervous. It even had a door under the stairs leading to the basement.

When I had been in Pasadena for about four months, my wife came out to visit. However, on the day that she arrived I was asked to travel right across the country to look for locations with the director and Mike, so I had no choice but to leave her in Pasadena.

However, it was the start of an amazing journey, from South Carolina to North Carolina, up to Detroit, through parts of Chicago and across to North Dakota – where I even saw a herd of buffalo – then on to Montana, Nevada, San Francisco and back to Los Angeles. It was such a shame that this film didn't get made, as the locations were wonderful.

On one trip somewhere in the mountains, we were looking for what the director described as an 'overlook view'. There were six of us on the recce and we were following a map (long before sat nav) and taking it in turns to drive when the director spotted what looked like a suitable place. The only trouble was that it meant going up a very narrow road with a drop-off to our left and a deep ditch to our right. Halfway up, there was a sign saying 'not suitable for motor vehicles' and we were in what can only be described as a mini-bus. However, intrepid heroes that we were, we carried on to our destination.

We found the overlook and it was superb – exactly what we wanted. Mike was going to drive back down and he started to do a three-point turn so that we were facing the right way but obviously misjudged it and the vehicle tipped into the ditch, blocking the passenger side so the only way out was through the driver's door. Given that this was a very remote place, we decided to split into twos to look for help, the youngest and the eldest staying with the vehicle, two going further up the mountain and two making their way down – which was Mike and myself. It was chilly with a promise of snow in the air, very quiet and very spooky.

On the way down I mentioned to Mike that I thought this was bear country. He agreed and wondered how we would protect ourselves if we were confronted. 'With a gun,' I said, but we didn't have one. At that point we thankfully saw lights coming towards us. It was a nice lady who offered to help. She turned her vehicle around, obviously very familiar with the road and a better driver than any of us, and took us down to the main road where there was a 7-Eleven supermarket with a gas station. There weren't many people about but there was plenty of food and we were really hungry by that

On the recce in the USA for *Lone Wolf and Cub*.

time. When Mike went to pay he asked if there might be someone with a breakdown truck to help us out and was told that the man was just finishing his tea and would be about half an hour. When he arrived he took us back to the vehicle and we found it out of the ditch and facing downhill, surrounded by a group of Boy Scouts who had manhandled it out of its predicament. It turned out that the pair who had gone up the hill had found a scout camp just around the next bend. How lucky! We spent the night in a local motel and continued our journey the next day.

We travelled over trestle bridges and around waterfalls, eventually reaching the Grand Canyon and Dead Horse Point, where the Colorado River has cut a series of curved amphitheatres around a peninsula. It was quite an impressive sight.

The director wanted to build a house on a hill that had to burn to the ground, similar to a scene in *Gone with the Wind*. We spotted a suitable hill and went into the field, not thinking about getting permission. In true western style, a man on a horse, chewing tobacco and toting a gun, rode across the field and asked what we were doing trespassing on his land. We explained very politely what we were about and he was, thankfully, very helpful but asked us firmly but nicely to leave. I must say, for a film that never was, this was a great experience with a lot of good memories.

The Mercenaries

Directed by Baron Lord Tyson, this was filmed in Beirut, where there was a lot of bomb damage from previous conflicts. They had employed a Lebanese art director who wasn't working out so I was called in. He was apparently supposed to dress a house out as reasonably well-to-do with period furniture but he had gone to the local dump and picked up whatever he could, so it didn't quite fit the bill!

I said that I needed at least $10,000, which I was given, and I went around all the antique shops getting furniture and accessories on a sale-or-return basis, with a commission of 10 per cent to the shop when the goods were returned.

A typical bomb-damaged area that we used as a set.

Because I was called in last minute I didn't have my normal crew with me so I had to use local labour. This made the job quite difficult as they had very little idea and very few tools. I asked for a mirror to be hung on a particular wall and when I returned I couldn't see it at first, as it was 15ft up. When I asked why it was so high they said that that was the nearest hook!

I was taken to a very damaged area with collapsed buildings and shrapnel hits. We went from one collapsed roof to another looking for suitable set-ups, with no harnesses on, just a rope around the waist, helped by a special effects man.

One scene needed a tank to go through the wall of a warehouse so we made a hole in the wall and filled it with breeze blocks, loosely bound with soft mortar so that they collapsed easily.

Blowing up a building in Beirut (not really, just explosions and smoke!).

We also had a tank break through a barrier and a scene where a row of tanks were firing dummy shells out to sea. It nearly started another war as no one had thought to advise the authorities so they sent a drone over to check it out, thought it was a real attack and scrambled two jets. That's what I call a proper action shot!

There was also a shot of a tank blowing up and setting on fire. The selected area was a car park, which we dressed with lorryloads of rubble. Obviously, the tank was a mock-up: a metal frame clad mostly with MDF, under the watchful eye of David Harris, the special effects supervisor. We had our fingers and everything else crossed but it went very well.

I remember going to look for a bomb-damaged village for one of the sequences. There were many to choose from but what I didn't realise at the time was that if you see a triangular sign with skull and crossbones it means 'No Entry – Unexploded Bombs'. The police arrived fairly quickly on the scene and asked me to turn around and retrace my footsteps. When I looked down there were so many prints in the dust I didn't know which were mine, but I did get back in one piece.

The local crew building the mock-up tank.

Lowering the mock-up tank into position on the set.

Me in a cheeky snap with
the interpreter!

Me with some of the cast
and crew.

Final instructions on set with the director Baron Lord Tyson (in the pink shirt) and the first assistant director.

The Mercenaries cast and crew on set and ready for action.

One location that was considered was an area full of boulders but we were advised by the local guide not to step in between the boulders as, again, there were mines there. Obviously the location wasn't suitable. When I asked how they would get rid of the mines they said they'd just send a herd of goats in. I think this production was never finished as it proved a little too dangerous for the cast and crew to continue filming.

Jack the Ripper

Another film that was never to reach the silver screen was *Jack the Ripper*. The whole thing was a very strange experience! While I was on the plane to Los Angeles for meetings, the producers decided to shoot the film in Australia using an Australian designer, so they no longer had any need for my services. Apparently the reason was that they wanted cobblestoned streets, which England didn't have – who knew! Having just worked on *Inspector Morse* in Oxford, I pointed out that there were quite a few cobbled streets there, as well as in many other towns and cities in the UK.

Another reason they gave was that they didn't like London's 'pea-souper' fogs, which, of course, had disappeared many years ago when central heating came into being. They had also been told that British crews were always having tea breaks and, as most studios had a bar, the crews did a lot of drinking. I tried to explain that the tea trolley was always on hand so that the crew could have a cuppa while still working and that the bars were used more for networking so that you could find out first-hand which films were hiring and who was available for work, with everyone keeping their eyes and ears open for the next job opportunity.

I think that the move to Australia was purely financial and they were just making excuses. Maybe I had a lucky escape in that I didn't have to waste more time on the project.

A FEW TECHNICAL EXPLANATIONS

As I was reading through the chapters, I realised that I was mentioning terms and procedures that are commonly used in the production process and might be familiar, but you may not be fully aware of how they work and how many other tricks and illusions are used in film production.

Many of the techniques that started in the early days are still used today, although most of what used to be called 'in-camera effects' (which required the animation of inanimate objects) have been superseded by digital visual effects inserted in the post-production stage. This is why, instead of using the original special effects designation, which covered almost everything, we now have to make a firm distinction between digital visual effects, which are completed in post-production, and special physical effects, which covers action shots and a lot of second unit work.

In-camera effects were complicated manoeuvres devised by specialist cameramen that involved many passes of the same film through the camera. One of the better proponents of this art was a very talented man called Gillie Potter, a magician of advertising in the early years of commercial television whose work often prompted viewers to wonder, 'How did they do that?' In fact, he and others like him managed to make those ads look digital before digital was invented. During the Second World War, Potter worked with the

Army Film and Photographic Unit. He was posted to Mountbatten's South East Asia Command, where he stayed after the war ended to help in setting up the Malaysian Government Film Unit, returning to the UK just in time for the start of ITV. He created rigs with rotating projectors, shape-changing items using progressively graduated bottles and glasses and, where liquid had to be poured in a constant stream and therefore had to be filmed in real time, yet another totally unique rig.

Another thing we, as film makers, assume is that everyone knows about the breadth of talent and diversity of job profiles involved in feature film production. Here we go on a very brief tour of the average film crew and the skills they bring to the project.

It all starts with the producer, who obtains a script or the rights to a book that they think will give a good financial return. A producer might have four or five treatments on the go at any one time and each one might take several years to come to fruition. The producer is backed up by a fully functional production office: assistant, associate and executive producers, production manager, production coordinator, line producer and financial controller. All of these jobs require many years of experience in the film industry as many millions of dollars or pounds are on the line.

You'll often hear the terms 'above the line' and 'below the line' when budgets are referred to. In general accounting, the line may separate operating income from other expenses. In film production 'above the line' generally refers to those such as the producer, director, production designer, director of photography and performers – the well-known names whose involvement with the film will encourage maximum financial support. You will often see in the credits the names of the stars next to the title 'executive producer', which also adds to the worth of the production. 'Below the line' means the rest of the film crew, who work for the various department heads to create the substance of the film.

Within this below-the-line budget, the art department budget is the largest. It is separated from the rest as it accommodates not only the draughtsmen but also the whole of the set construction and the materials that will be needed to build all the sets, both in the studio and on location.

Next comes the director. They are in charge of the creative production 'army' – both cast and crew. They choose the heads of department who are going to work with them for the duration of the production and post-production processes, and who they know will suit the style of the film. These are the production designer, director of photography, post-production supervisor, hair and make-up designer, costume designer, sound designer and, hopefully, if they're a good director, the music supervisor, as we all know how important the theme and background music are to the enjoyment and appreciation of the film. Each one of these heads of department comes complete with their own tried and tested crews.

Now we come to my sector of the production process, the art department. As head of the department, the production designer will know exactly which art director and construction manager they want to work with on a particular job, who will both come as a complete package with their own dedicated teams. The art department is the largest workforce on any film and therefore warrants its own budget. Given that this department also includes the full construction crew, the workforce can number up to 200 or 300 people involved both in the studio and on location, with all the materials and equipment needed to build as many sets as required. You can understand why the financial controller wants this budget to be separate from the rest in order that it can be better monitored.

The production designer, having worked with the producer and director to understand what is required, will pass sketches and designs for the sets to the art director, and the process begins. The draughtsmen in the art department produce blueprints and detailed drawings, which go to the construction manager and the team of scenic carpenters, ornamental plasterers, scenic painters, sculptors and riggers who will build the sets. All of these extremely skilled craftsmen and -women have to be able to understand the complex drawings and specifications, so they need a good grasp of physics and mathematics. Many sets are not just a façade but have to function as real buildings with all the load-bearing and safety aspects needed to support people, animals and vehicles.

Once finished, the sets have to be dressed. In come the set dresser, props, drapes, greens (trees and ornamental plants, both real and fabricated) and, on action films, vehicles, guns, tanks or whatever the director calls for. There are so many specialist people and suppliers involved to support the production at every stage. On set the standby art director is always available to deal with any problems and is essentially the liaison between what's happening on the floor and the designer and art director.

Now to explain some of the procedures and tricks of the trade involved in my particular area, many of which I've mentioned throughout the book.

As a major head of department, the production designer is right there at the beginning, working closely with the director, art director, construction manager, costume designer, hair and make-up designer and director of photography, all of whom play a crucial role in helping the producer and director to achieve the visual requirements of the film.

Working from the script and/or screenplay, you have to assess the visual qualities that will create the right atmosphere on set for the performers to bring the story to life. With the director and director of photography you'll discuss how best to shoot the film – whether to use studio sets and/or locations, what should be built and what could be adapted, whether there is a visual theme that recurs throughout the film, whether there are certain design elements that may give an emotional depth to the film and when and where special physical effects and visual effects (CGI) should be used.

As art director you are essentially the project manager of the art department. You have to fully understand how sets and props will interact with the cast as well as with lighting, special effects and camera action. On top of this you have to manage the budget and crew, often over multiple studio sets and locations. It can be quite intense but also very exciting and rewarding. I must say that I think I have learned something fresh almost every day that I've gone to work!

The draughtsmen (drafters in the USA) convert the sketches into detailed technical drawings to give visual and structural guidelines to the construction crew, specifying dimensions and materials with additional drawings, sketches, specifications and calculations. They have to be fully aware of standard building techniques, creative enough to adapt the designer's concept into a very practical form and able to accommodate action sequences and imaginary elements for science-fiction and fantasy films. As well as being very conversant with the scope of camera lenses, matte shots and set layout, these clever people will be able to produce their drawings with either pencil and drawing board or current digital technology such as CAD and other software products.

As well as the drawings, draughtsmen will very often be asked to provide card models. These are 3D 'sketches' constructed in cardboard to help the director and the director of photography plan their shots in advance of the build and check if any structural elements will get in the way of the action and the camera angles. This is where discussions are had with the art director to see if any walls may have to be removed during shooting and therefore need to be built as breakaways (destroyable or removable scenery), and to address other such technical issues. These models can also be constructed using a variety of computer software but many still prefer to work with physical card models. These models are not to be confused with miniatures, which are also sometimes referred to as models, particularly in the USA.

My brother, production designer Brian Ackland-Snow, showing director Alfonso Arau a white-card model on the set of *The Magnificent Ambersons*.

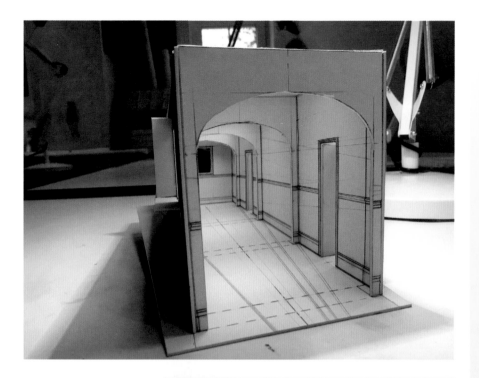

This page: Sections of a white card-model under construction, with a figure showing the perspectives that will be required for the set build.

Opposite: Aspects of the interior of a finished card model.

A white-card model of a street exterior.

Opposite: Aspects of the interior of a finished card model.

Miniatures are one of the most used physical 'illusions' across the board of film, television and adverts. This innocuous word covers a multitude of extraordinary tricks used to create a world of different dimensions that, combined with skilled camerawork, fools the eye into believing what is observed is real.

The miniatures builder works with all types of wood, metal, plastics, fibreglass and other casting materials. The idea is to fabricate a three-dimensional scale model, which can be anything from two-thirds life-size to tiny models for an animation set.

The miniature builder's job spans the art, effects (both physical and digital), camera and construction departments, but they mainly work under the instruction of the visual effects supervisor. They make model sets of venues that may be too expensive to hire for the shoot – a stately home or theatre, a historical ship that no longer exists – or perhaps something that needs to be destroyed as part of the action.

The process for constructing models and miniatures begins long before the shoot is scheduled to take place. Instructions can be as simple as rough sketches or as complex as specific designs. The miniatures builder not only has to work out how their models will look on film but also to make sure that they are historically and culturally accurate.

Then there are a lot of questions to be asked. How will the miniature be used? Will it be 'as is' or a background detail, perhaps seen through a window or as a replacement in a composite shot? Will it be filmed with live-action components combined in-camera or will the components be put together in post-production? Will it be filmed as a static build, as a mobile or with mobile elements? If mobile, which parts move and in what direction? How will the mobiles be driven – electric motor or string and sealing wax? What about explosions, floods or fire? Does it have to collapse? Does it have to float or sink? If so, does the build need to be flexible to allow rapid changes on set to compensate for damage or to do a second and third take?

Budget permitting, the scale may range greatly. Given the intricacies of some miniatures, it's very often less expensive to create a larger model. Using a smaller scale could also mean extremely high camera speeds, which can be tricky and time-consuming. Often the larger miniatures are called 'bigatures'!

Left and opposite: A miniature – or 'bigature' – under construction on location, then prepared for a night shoot. *(Courtesy of Leigh Took, Mattes & Miniatures VFX Ltd)*

Matte painting is one of the earliest techniques used to composite additional images onto footage and it is still used today. If a scene is to be filmed in a not-so-perfect location, a large piece of painted glass or Perspex would be used as a mask between the camera and the action. The glass is positioned so that it fills the camera frame and is far enough away to be held in focus, with the background visible through it. The entire scene is painted on the glass, except for the area where the action is to take place, which is left clear. Filmed through the glass, the live action is composited with the painted area, thus creating a seamless sequence.

Hanging miniatures are suspended or placed between the camera and the live set so as to appear as part of the set when seen by the camera. They often serve the same purpose as the glass or matte painting but they have a more three-dimensional quality, which gives a greater depth to the scene and makes the illusion more realistic.

Leigh Took up on an 80ft tower painting a matte on glass in Pinewood Studios. *(Courtesy of Leigh Took, Mattes & Miniatures VFX Ltd)*

Opposite page: A miniature of a church roof being built on a stage, then lit and ready for action. *(Courtesy of Leigh Took, Mattes & Miniatures VFX Ltd)*

This brings us nicely into 'forced perspective', which is a technique used not only for filming miniatures but also when shooting a scene in a studio that may have much less space than needed. Sometimes this is necessary due to a schedule change, or perhaps additional shots are needed after the crew has left the location. Technically, forcing the linear perspective causes the distance to be compressed. For example, in a street scene, the buildings will start to condense towards the end of the road and perhaps a ramp will be used to create a false horizon. Tricks of lighting and careful placement of props add to the illusion, which was originally copied from theatre sets.

If you wish to give the impression of a long corridor and you are restricted in stage space, it is often necessary to build a forced perspective section in the set. At the end of the section you can carry on the illusion of depth by using a painted backing in the correct position, or create it in post-production with CGI, although this is a much more expensive method.

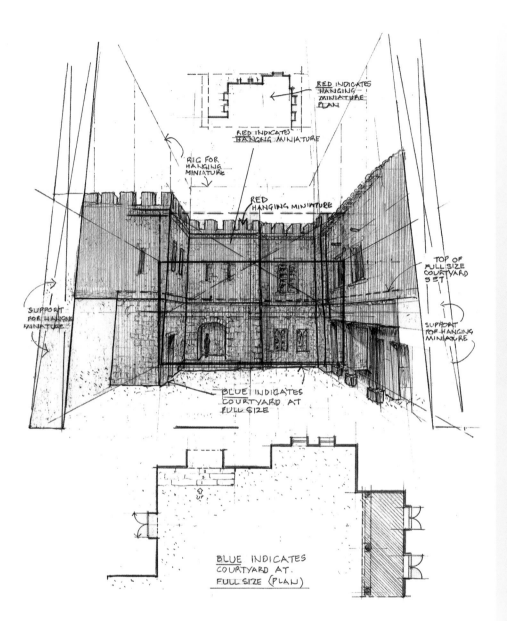

RED INDICATES HANGING MINIATURE PLAN

RED INDICATES HANGING MINIATURE

RIG FOR HANGING MINIATURE

RED HANGING MINIATURE

TOP OF FULL SIZE COURTYARD SET

SUPPORT FOR HANGING MINIATURE

SUPPORT FOR HANGING MINIATURE

BLUE INDICATES COURTYARD AT FULL SIZE

BLUE INDICATES COURTYARD AT FULL SIZE (PLAN)

Sketch showing how a full-sized set and hanging miniature work together. The blue section is the full-sized set on the ground and the pink section is the hanging miniature in the foreground.

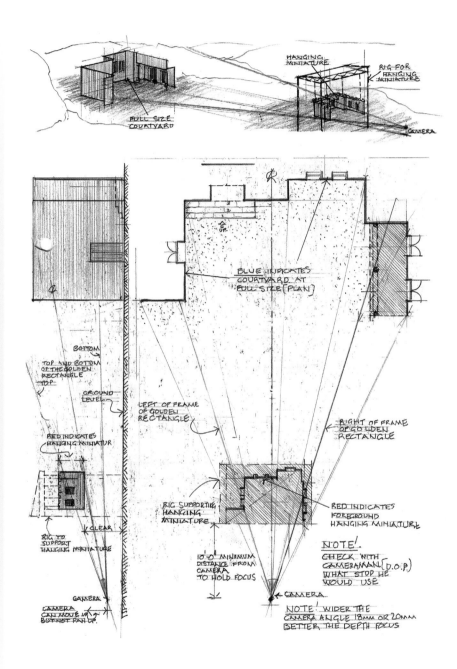

Overhead view of the hanging miniature set.

Now back to the art department! Imagine the drawings have gone to the construction manager. This is the person responsible for interpreting the designs and turning the blueprints into fully functional film sets. The construction crew functions more or less in the same way that a domestic building site does.

Starting from the ground up, the rigger is essentially a scaffolder with extended skills. They put up the essential structural skeletons to support the build. They also construct heavy mobile sets, handle the lighting rails and install lifting and suspension apparatus, as well as any platforms that the carpenters, plasterers, painters and scenic artists might need. They are not to be confused with the stagehands, who work alongside the construction, props and set-dressing teams, doing everything from hanging backdrops to taking care of transport. They are essentially a 'Mr Fix-it' on set.

The scenic carpenters, joiners and painters have to have all the skills and qualifications of the domestic variety but with so much more to offer. They are the bedrock of the construction crew. After the riggers have finished building the basis on which the sets are supported, the carpenters step in to build both the exteriors and interiors of the set. The scenery can include anything from flat walls and doors to highly involved projects such as an entire castle, a ship's cabin or a spaceship. If you want to see a plane on a runway, you don't necessarily have to have the real thing when a life-sized mock-up will do, as you can see from the photographs. The image the camera sees looks perfectly 'real' but if you look behind the façade it's all an illusion!

Next come the ornamental plasterers to flesh out the work done by the carpenters and take the set to another level. This is seen more as a craft rather than a trade because of the wide range of skills used. A full understanding of the chemicals involved is essential, combined with creativity and the ability to understand complex drawings and sketches.

The back view of an aeroplane on the runway showing construction. *(Courtesy of construction manager Terry Apsey)*

The front view of the same aeroplane painted and ready for the camera. *(Courtesy of construction manager Terry Apsey)*

Once the plasterers are done, the scenic painters take over. The range of expertise necessary to finish the set takes the word 'painter' to a whole new level. The work has to convince the audience that what they are looking at through the camera lens is real. I've walked onto a set and had to touch what appeared to be a marble pillar to see if was real or not – that's how convincing the work of the painters is! They are artists rather than decorators, with skills learned through many years' experience.

Above top: The back view of an aircraft hangar showing the same wood and scaffolding construction. *(Courtesy of construction manager Terry Apsey)*

Above bottom: The hangar and plane as seen by the camera. *(Courtesy of construction manager Terry Apsey)*

Scenic plasterers at work in the plaster shop creating columns.

This beautiful building in the Persian style is constructed of scaffolding, wood and plaster – amazing craftsmanship that takes many years to perfect. *(Courtesy of head of department plasterer Ken Barley)*

The scenic artists have a different job. They are artists who paint the backings and create any special portraits, murals and posters needed. Many have trained in the theatre so will have an extensive knowledge of all aspects of perspective, period styles and architecture.

The sculptors create anything from statues of all types and proportions to ornate panelling and specialised pieces for fantasy films. Polystyrene is generally the material of choice as it's lightweight and easy to transport.

Now we come to the set dresser or decorator (in television and adverts they are often called stylists). They step in to turn the blank canvas of the constructed set into a 'lived-in' space. They deal with dressing props such as wall hangings, drapes and flooring; hand props, which is anything picked up or used by the actors; hero props,

Again, this construction is scaffolding, wood, plaster and paint, finished by the scenic painters. The marbling and finishes are exquisite and it's hard to believe that this is just an illusion. *(Courtesy of head of department painter Adrian Start)*

which are central to the action; stunt props, which are soft replicas such as furniture or bottles that will be smashed; and mechanical props, which is anything that moves or is illuminated. This gives a sense of atmosphere and period to a set.

The property master and the team are responsible for any and all hired, manufactured or purchased props, including furniture, equipment, farm machinery and such like. Like the set dresser, they are generally on hand to make sure that the props are always in the right place at the right time for the action.

There are a lot of really talented people working very hard behind the scenes to make whatever the audience sees on the screen as enjoyable and believable as possible. The one thing we all have to be aware of in everything we do in the art department is what the camera is going to be looking at. Anyone who has taken a photograph knows that there's always a limit to how much you can fit into the lens at any one time. The framing is so important when you look at the picture you've snapped. From the beginning of their training, every draughtsman will start to absorb information about camera angles and perspective, so by the time they are able to take on the role of art director they will have a good working knowledge of cameras and lenses, both film and digital.

As you can see, working in the art department isn't just about drawing nice pictures, doing fancy stuff and travelling the world – although all of that does come into it. It's a complicated, challenging, highly technical job. It takes a lot of time, hard work, an adaptable spirit and a very understanding family to reach the dizzy heights of art director and production designer. However, I wouldn't change anything about my life in film. Looking back, I've laughed, cried and, above all, enjoyed all of it and, although I'm now retired, I'm really happy to be passing my knowledge on to the next generation of film makers.

INDEX

References to images are in *italics*.

The History Press
The destination for history
www.thehistorypress.co.uk